SIR ISAAC NEWTON

THEOLOGICAL MANUSCRIPTS

SIR ISAAC NEWTON
THEOLOGICAL MANUSCRIPTS

Selected and Edited with an Introduction by

H. McLACHLAN, M.A., D.D., Litt.D.

LIVERPOOL
AT THE UNIVERSITY PRESS
1950

C. Tinling & Co., Limited,

Printers,

Liverpool, London & Prescot.

PREFACE

THE manuscripts of Newton here printed are reproduced with certain differences. Contractions and abbreviations have been eliminated and words written in full ; the punctuation has been improved, and the spelling modernized, but quaint expressions, still intelligible, have been retained. Latin notes in the Common Place Book have been translated into English, but elsewhere Latin quotations, where the context elucidates their meaning, are given *verbatim et literatim*. Words in square brackets are not in the MSS.

Part I of the Introduction relates briefly the story of the fortunes of the MSS. from Newton's death to the present time, whilst Part II attempts to trace the development and sketch the character of Newton's theology. Both are to some extent dependent upon the MSS. to which references are made.

The Hibbert Trust is responsible for the publication of the manuscripts, but not for opinions expressed in the Introduction to them. Thanks are tendered to the Provost and Council of King's College for permission to print them, and to Mr. K. Povey, M.A., Librarian of Liverpool University, for their safe keeping in the Harold Cohen Library during their use. Mr. R. Angus Downie, Secretary of the Liverpool University Press, has given invaluable assistance in seeing the book through the press.

Liverpool, 1949. H. McLachlan

FOREWORD

THE Hibbert Trustees, who are responsible for the publication
of this volume, express their gratitude to the Provost and
Council of King's College, Cambridge, for the permission to
publish the ten Theological Manuscripts, hitherto unpublished,
which are dealt with in this book, and for their willingness to
allow these Manuscripts to be deposited, for the convenience of
Dr. H. McLachlan, the Editor of the volume, at the Liverpool
University Library. They are also indebted to the Librarian of
King's College Library for his courtesy and helpfulness in the
effecting of the temporary transfer, and to the Librarian of the
Liverpool University Library for undertaking the safe keeping of
the Manuscripts.

CONTENTS

INTRODUCTION

I. *The Newton Theological Manuscripts*

S IR ISAAC NEWTON was born 25 December, 1642, and died 20 March, 1727. During his lifetime he was known as an ardent Protestant suspected of heterodoxy, with a profound interest in theology, though he could never be persuaded to take orders. No theological work was published by him, though once at least he seems to have contemplated publication, for he begins the Introduction to a large MS. Treatise on the Book of Revelation with the words :

> Having searched after knowledge in the prophetic scriptures, I have thought myself bound to communicate it for the benefit of others, remembering the judgment of him who hid his talent in a napkin.[1]

Prophetic and apocalyptic studies were not wont to evoke censure in Newton's day, but his were animated by anti-Romanism and, to use his favourite cliché, "by consequence" anti-episcopalianism. Realisation of what might be involved by this and, even more, by his investigations of primitive church discipline, the origins of Christian dogmas, and their assumed sources in Scripture, induced in him an extra caution, strengthened by dislike of controversy, and by devotion to duty in state and university, whose performance might have been imperilled by the publication of his theological manuscripts.

The number, character, and, occasionally, the length of these manuscripts are amazing. Their subjects include Chronology, Apocalyptic Literature, Church History, Prophecy, Ecclesiastical Polity, The Nature and Content of Religion, The Relation of Jews and Christians, Roman Catholicism, The Sibylline Oracles, Solomon's Temple, Trinitarianism, New Testament Textual Criticism ; and to these he added copious extracts from the Bible, patristic literature and early ecclesiastical historians. According to Professor Andrade's estimate, " there were over 1,300,000 words in MSS. on theology in the Portsmouth Collection."

[1] See Luke xix, 20f ; Matthew xxv, 25f.

Probably no one has read all these manuscripts, and many of them have little value in the light of modern scholarship, but that is by no means true of all.

As early as 1680 Newton discussed prophecy with Henry More, and in 1690 sent Locke a valuable treatise[1] on two important doctrinal texts upon which he had been at work for some time.   A MS. note in Latin reveals the fact that long before he sent it, he had studied one of the texts, and used a volume published in 1669, written by a learned Arian scholar in Prussia and sent to the press by his son in Holland.

Within eighteen days of Newton's death, on 7 April, 1727, his friend John Craig (d. 1731) gave an account of the Newton manuscripts on theology.

> This I know that he (Sir Isaac Newton) was much more solicitous in his enquiries into Religion than into Natural Philosophy . . . Sir Isaac Newton, to make his inquiries into the Christian religion more successful, had read the ancient writers and ecclesiastical historians with great exactness, and had drawn up in writing great collections out of both[2] and to show how earnest he was in religion, he had written a long explication of remarkable parts of the Old and New Testaments[2], while his understanding was in its greatest perfection, lest the infidels might pretend that his applying himself to the study of religion was the effect of dotage. That he would not publish these writings in his own time, because they showed that his thoughts were sometimes different from those which are commonly received, which would engage him in dispute ; and this was a thing which he avoided as much as possible.   But now it's hoped that the worthy and ingenious Mr. Conduitt will take care that they be published.

Dr. Thomas Pellett, F.R.S., was appointed by Newton's executor to examine the papers and determine what ought to be sent to the press. This was begun in May, 1727.   On the inner cover of a large Common Place Book, devoted mainly to theological subjects, is the inscription : "Sep. 25, 1727, Not fit to be printed. Tho. Pellett." His report on the papers was so condemnatory as to lead Whiston immediately[3] to defy him to make good his accusations.   " I

[1] An Account of Two Notable Corruptions of Scripture.
[2] In the Common Place Book.
[3] *Authentick Records*, II, 1076 (1727).

conjure him on the peril of being charged with open falsehood and forgery, if he continue that report, to take care that those original papers, from which he pretends to collect that imputation, be ready to be produced under Sir Isaac's hand for his justification." No reply to this challenge was forthcoming. The only result of Pellett's examination was that Conduitt published late in 1727 (title date 1728) Newton's *Chronology of Ancient Kingdoms*, edited by Pellett and Martin Folkes, F.R.S. ; which was followed in 1733 by his *Observations upon the Prophecies of Daniel and the Apocalypse of St. John*, edited by a son of Newton's half-brother. These works, now of little value, reveal few traces of the heretical opinions credited to Newton by his friends, William Whiston and Hopton Haynes, the first, his successor in the chair at Cambridge, the second, his assistant at the Mint.

Catharine Conduitt, née Barton, Newton's favourite niece, who had lived with him many years, cannot have been satisfied with the outcome of this examination, for she resolved upon the publication of at least some of the more important manuscripts. With the contents of these she may possibly have been acquainted, or, more probably from all we know of her, she was aware of her husband's or uncle's high opinion of them. Accordingly, in the codicil to her last Will and Testament, 26 January, 1737, she ordained that " my Executor do lay all the tracts relating to Divinity before Dr. Sykes, in hopes he will prepare them for the press." She then named " The Historical Account," " Paradoxical Questions concerning Athanasius," " A History of the Creed," " A Church History," and " Many Divinity Tracts," adding, " the papers must be carefully kept, that no copies may be taken and printed and Dr. Sykes to peruse them here," i.e., at her residence, Cranbury Park, Hants. Alas, John Conduitt died 23 May, 1737, and his wife 20 January, 1739. Their only child, Catharine, married 8 March, 1740, John Wallop, Viscount Lymington, son of the first Earl of Portsmouth, and Newton's manuscripts passed into the possession of the Portsmouth family at Hurstbourne Park, North Hants. When, more than fifteen years after Mrs. Conduitt's death, Dr. Sykes was approached, in tardy accordance with her Will, he was probably unable to make the journey from London to Hampshire. This seems to be the meaning of the MS. note " An Acc^t of Sir Isaac Newton's papers sent to the Rev^d Dr. Sikes (sic) to London, 12 Nov., 1755." He was then a sick man and may never have seen them, for he died from paralysis 23 November, 1756.

Mrs. Conduitt's appointment of the final arbiter in the choice of manuscripts for publication is noteworthy. Arthur Ashley Sykes was a latitudinarian divine who argued that the Church had no uniform doctrine, and that members of it were not obliged to agree in opinion. He was a stalwart supporter of Dr. Samuel Clarke, the Arian philosopher, who in 1706 translated Newton's *Optics* into Latin, and later defended his philosophy against Leibnitz. John Disney, D.D., an ex-clergyman and later Unitarian minister of Essex Street Chapel, " a careful and exact writer", in his *Memoirs of the Life and Writings of Arthur Ashley Sykes, D.D.* (1785), makes no mention of the Newton manuscripts. Had Dr. Sykes " perused " them and published those he approved immediately after Mrs. Conduitt's death, it is safe to say many would have been printed about 1740, as she intended them to be.

Some manuscripts, including that of " An Historical Account of Two Notable Corruptions of the Scriptures," were given by Lady Lymington to her executor, Mr. Jeffrey Ekins, from whom they passed successively into the hands of the Dean of Carlisle (d. 1791) and the Rev. Jeffrey Ekins, rector of Sampford, who possessed them in 1855 when Brewster saw " copies of many of them." As early as 1837 he began his examination of the manuscripts in the Portsmouth Collection. The ban on copying and printing of manuscripts, made by Mrs. Conduitt in 1737 in order that Dr. Sykes alone should determine what should be published, was plainly continued for other reasons by the clerical family into whose hands some of them fell. Happily, the MS. of " An Historical Account " they owned was not the only one known, and the text of that formerly in the hands of Locke was edited and published anonymously in 1759. In October, 1777, Horsley saw all the manuscripts when preparing his edition of Newton's *Works*, 1779-1785, and, reluctantly we may well believe, included the treatise on the Two Texts, as he says, " from a MS. in the possession of the Rev. Dr. Ekins, Dean of Carlisle." The full story of the MSS. of " An Historical Account " has been told elsewhere.[1]

In 1795 a rough catalogue of Newton's papers was printed by Charles Hutton, F.R.S., in his *Mathematical and Philosophical Dictionary*. He observed :

It is astonishing what care and industry Sir Isaac Newton had employed on the papers relating to Chronology, Church

[1] *Religious Opinions of Milton, Locke and Newton* (1941) pp. 131ff., by the writer.

History, etc., which are in the possession of the family of the Earl of Portsmouth. . . Many of them copies over and over again . . . upwards of four thousand sheets . . .

Clearly, the manuscripts, many of them written out with corrections and additions several times, must represent work done over a considerable period. Manuscripts of "An Historical Account"—of the two texts and of each one separately—were circulated by Newton amongst his friends, and one on the second text (I Timothy III, 16) fell into the hands of an unfriendly critic, John Berriman, who did not know who wrote it. Dr. Abraham Rees was therefore right in his surmise, published in Lord King's *Life of John Locke* (1829), that besides the manuscript sent to Locke in 1691, Newton " at a later period must have written many other copies. . ." From the catalogue of the Newton Manuscripts at Lord Portsmouth's at Hurstbourne Park, it would appear that there are some copies there ; but whether in a perfect state or not, cannot be ascertained until that collection shall have been examined by some competent person, less influenced by theological and ecclesiastical biases, than the learned and Right Reverend editor of Sir Isaac Newton's Works."[1]

Amongst the unpublished MSS. is a note on I John v, 7, in the Common Place Book ; also " Corruptelae Duorum Celebrium in Sacris Literis Historia Narratio,' Amstelodami, Anno 1709", " not in Newton's hand, but containing a few autograph corrections. It is a Latin version of the first part of the ' Historical Account ' (i.e., of the first text), but is complete, ending with the word ' Finis,' and is rather longer than the English text," that is, the text published by Horsley. This is almost certainly a Latin translation made by Hopton Haynes, which Alexander Gordon[2] dates "after 1708." He also states that Hopton Haynes's " entrance into the Mint was nearly synchronous with Sir Isaac Newton's appointment as Warden (19 March, 1696), and it is not improbable that he was a protegé of Newton with whom he was very intimate till Newton's death." This is confirmed by a MS. " Draft of a Letter, Autograph, to the Lords of Treasury, supporting Hopton Haynes's petition for the office of Weigher and Teller of the Mint," and also of one giving Haynes's petition for the office.

In 1728 Whiston wrote[3] : " These Dissertations were both put

[1] Lord King, *Life of Locke* (1829), i, 434.
[2] *D.N.B. s.v.*
[3] *Authentick Records*, Part II, 1077.

into Latin by a common friend of Sir I. N's and mine (elsewhere identified as Haynes) many years ago, by Sir I. N's desire, and, I suppose, with a design to have them printed. . . . They were not printed at that time, and are now in the hands of Sir I. N's executors." Hopton Haynes himself, writing as early as 1747[1], after referring to the persecution of Thomas Emlyn for his Unitarian opinions, said : " The spirit of Popery is not quite exorcised. It kept in awe, and silenced some extraordinary persons amongst us, Sir P(eter) K(ing), Sir J(oseph) J(ekyl), and the greatest man of the age, and glory of the British Nation, I mean, the renowned Sir I(saac) N(ewton), who, amongst other MSS., has left behind him a short discourse upon the pretended text of St. John, which (with others now in the hands of a noble Lord) will, 'tis hoped, be published in convenient time." None of Newton's biographers exhibit any acquaintance with the doctrinal writings of Haynes, an intimate friend of Henry Hedworth, one of the circle of Unitarian Tract Writers, who named Hopton Haynes in his Will. Bishop Horsley, the brilliant but unscrupulous opponent of Priestley, in the incomplete list of Newton's MSS. in his edition of Newton's Works, mentions a Latin translation of " An Historical Account " without the name of the translator. Possibly he did not know it ; more probably he could not bring himself to mention a zealous Unitarian whose posthumous work, *The Scripture Account of the Worship of God and the Offices of Jesus Christ* (1750) ran to four editions, the second (1790) being edited, with a Preface, by Theophilus Lindsey, Priestley's friend, and published by the Unitarian Society.

In 1835, in the *Life and Correspondence of John Flamsteed*, the first Astronomer Royal (d. 1719), Francis Baily declared that he had access to the unpublished works of Newton in the family of the Earl of Portsmouth, pronounced them most important, and hinted at the possibility of at least a part of these valuable remains being published under the auspices of the Government, provided the consent of certain persons, in whose custody they remain, can be obtained. These, it is said, appear divided on the subject. Ultimately their verdict must have been in the negative.

Sir David Brewster wrote the *Life of Newton*, 1831, apparently without any knowledge of the manuscripts, and did not hesitate to affirm that Newton was a believer in the Trinity. Subsequently, many

[1] *Causa Dei contra Novatores; or The Religion of the Bible and the Pulpit Compared*, p. 31.

writers, at home and abroad, followed him in acclaiming the orthodoxy of the great scientist. In 1837, Brewster examined the manuscripts, and in *Memoirs of Sir Isaac Newton*, 2 vols., 1855 ; 2nd ed. 1860, he qualified his former judgment so far as to admit that Newton's orthodoxy was not proved, " but in the charity which thinketh no evil, we are bound to believe that our neighbour is not a heretic till the charge against him has been distinctly proved." Horsley had been responsible for the report that Newton left behind him a cartload of papers on religious subjects, which he had examined and found unfit for publication, after which he asserted, in a comment on a passage in " An Historical Account," that the writer " was not a Socinian," meaning at that date " not a Unitarian." Still Brewster thought " Dr. Horsley exercised a wise discretion in not giving other manuscripts formally to the world." He himself did far from justice to the manuscript evidence of Newton's heresies. He printed a few selected papers, at least in part, but not those most important for the determination of Newton's personal beliefs.

Not until 1934 did any adequate survey of the Newton theological manuscripts appear in print. In that year was published the comprehensive and scientific biography of Newton, written by Professor L. T. More, of Cincinnati University, U.S.A. It cannot be regarded as the last word on the subject of Newton's theology but it proves conclusively that in many ways, and not alone in his interpretation of Newton's religious opinions, Brewster as a biographer is untrustworthy. After a critical discussion of the manuscripts for the first time, More concludes that " Newton was an Arian."

In July, 1936, at the sale of the Newton Papers by order of Viscount Lymington, Lord Keynes, we are told[1], " attended the sale in person, and bought about forty lots, but this was only a fraction of his ultimate acquisition from this collection." He managed gradually to reassemble about half of the collection, including the whole of the biographical portion, that is, the ' Conduitt Papers '."

Lord Keynes died 21 April, 1946. In July that year at the Tercentenary Celebrations by the Royal Society (published 1947), a lecture on " Newton, The Man," which Keynes had prepared before

---

[1] *The Times Literary Supplement*, Oct. 19, 1946. Art. " Lord Keynes and his Books," by A. N. L. Munby.

1942, was read by his brother, Mr. Geoffrey Keynes, the distinguished surgeon and bibliographer. In the same year (1946) it was announced that Lord Keynes's library, including the Newton Collection, was bequeathed to King's College, Cambridge. Early in 1948, by kind permission of the Provost and Council of the College, the Hibbert Trustees were enabled to place a number of selected theological manuscripts on deposit for a period in the Harold Cohen Library, Liverpool University, for the purpose of examination with a view to publication.

In the Lovelace Collection of Locke's Papers (purchased for the Bodleian Library, Oxford, in 1948) are Journals, Letters, and Note Books. His Common Place Book, of which some use was made by Lord King in 1829, still remains in private possession. It was Locke's practice, we are told, [1] "to enter in his note-books excerpts from the books he read and drafts of the treatises he wrote," which " establishes the fact that the subjects discussed by him in the writings he published from 1690 onwards had been occupying his mind for 20 or 30 years." It is as remarkable that Locke's MSS. should come into the possession of the Oxford Library so soon after the Newton MSS. were presented to the Cambridge College as it is interesting to discover that two friends, whose opinions on politics and religion were much the same, adopted the same methods of note-taking and gave many years' study to preparation for possible publication of their work.

More than a century ago a discerning scholar wrote[2] " In an age when old opinions were fearlessly cast aside, and the freest stimulus was given to the pursuit of truth . . . its two greatest philosophers—the one leading on the van of moral science, the other conducting discovery with unexampled triumphs through the physical creation—stood firmly and devotedly by the religion of Jesus Christ : not simply paying it the respectful homage due to a venerable and beneficent belief, but subjecting its history and documents to a thoughtful scrutiny, and consecrating their high powers to its illustration and defence."

---

[1] *The Times,* January 12, 1948. Art. " John Locke's Papers."

[2] J. J. Tayler. *Retrospect of the Religious Life of England* (1845) pp. 361-2.

II. NEWTON'S THEOLOGY

Its Development and Character

A POSTHUMOUS child, with a stepfather and an uncle in holy orders, Newton spent his early years in the religious atmosphere of the Church of England. After an elementary education in two village schools, at the age of twelve he entered the Grantham Grammar School. Here he spent five years, 1654-58 (from twelve to sixteen), then after a break, another year, 1660-61 (eighteen), residing throughout with Apothecary Clark, a good churchman, with whose step-daughter he fell in love. Under a picture in his room were said to be lines by him attributing to the " Martyr King " the traditional piety credited to him by his faithful followers. Professor More, accepting the sketch and verse as the work of Newton[1], not only deduces that " the boy was brought up in a family devoted to the Church of England the Royal cause," but also that " he was opposed to the prevalent sympathy of the countryside to Cromwell, the more significant because, in later life, he became a convinced Whig and Anti-Jacobin."

Professor Andrade, however, points out[2] that " the verses attributed to Newton were taken by him from the ' Eikon Basilike[3],' where they appear under a picture of Charles I which he copied." It may be significant that the story of Newton's sketching comes ultimately from Clark, and that of the verse, repeated from memory, from his step-daughter. Even if Newton reproduced both, the copies were probably no more than a tribute by a swain to his beloved and her family. A young man in love does not necessarily disclose his own religious and political sentiments in the use to which he puts pen and pencil as a copyist, especially one so secretive and reserved as Newton. The affair between the two came to nothing. Newton never married ; the lady married twice.

[1] *Isaac Newton A Biography* (1934), p. 15.

[2] *Newton Centenary Celebrations* (1946), p. 15.

[3] " Eikon Basilike," purporting to be meditations by King Charles, were published shortly after his execution (1649), and accepted by Royalists as genuine. It was written by John Gauden (1603-62), afterwards Bishop of Worcester.

B

There is no evidence that in early manhood Newton underwent any conversion in his religious and political opinions.   More himself affirms[1] : " It is clear to me that Newton had been deeply affected by the Protestantism of the Commonwealth from 1642 to 1660," that is to say, a period of which he spent five years, at an impressionable age, in Grantham, where Puritan influences upon him, unnoticed by his biographers, were by no means wanting.

The officiating ministers of the church he attended were Henry Vaughan and John Starkey.   Henry Vaughan[2] had been at Oxford, left without graduating, and was ordained by the Manchester Classis, 15 April, 1647, at Moreton Say, Salop.   He was imprisoned first at Grantham and later at Lincoln, for refusing to read the prayer book.   He was ejected from Grantham in 1662.   Richard Baxter described him in 1671 as " a worthy minister, lately discouraged." Next year he was licensed as a Presbyterian.   John Starkey, lecturer at Grantham, was. a Cambridge graduate, who, after ejection, removed to Lancashire, was licensed as a Presbyterian at Ormskirk in 1672, and was minister at Newington Green, 1686-1692[3].   By his Will, 11 June, 1692, he left £50 towards the maintenance of " such Nonconforming ministers who preach the Holy Word of God to people that are able to contribute but Little to their maintenance." Baxter spoke of him as " an able, sober, judicious man of great worth."   Such were the men whom young Newton would hear on the Sabbath, and their doctrine respecting the authority of Scripture, church discipline, and ritual assuredly did not fall on deaf ears.

It is certain that Newton's posthumous works were intended to uphold Protestantism and combat the claims of the Roman Church. This zeal is confirmed by his numerous manuscripts on Scripture, Church History and Christian Doctrine.   For no man had he less respect than for Athanasius.   This is most apparent in " Paradoxical Questions concerning the morals and actions of Athanasius and his Followers," which presents a picture of the fourth century theologian unfamiliar to most students of early ecclesiastical history.   It is plain, too, from Newton's writings, that his authority in religion was the Bible, not General Councils, nor Convocations, nor even the Prayer Book, and, moreover, that like Ussher, Baxter, Locke, and the

[1] *Ut supra*, p. 629.
[2] A. G. Matthews, *Calamy Revised*, pp. 500-501.
[3] Matthews, *Calamy Revised*, p. 460.   Also Alex. Gordon, *Freedom After Ejection*, p. 353.

contemporary Unitarian Tract Writers, he stood for Comprehension in the National Church, whilst he went beyond most in his limited requirement of doctrinal profession as essential for church membership, and his advocacy of a primitive and democratic discipline. In a brief sketch of the Church, he speaks of Elders or Presbyters, Deacons and Presidents, and of cities as ecclesiastical territories " which together compose the Church Catholic."

The foundations for some at least of these convictions were laid at Grantham. There is more to be said.

More observes[1] : " Newton early acquired the habit of reading. His first source of reading lay in a parcel of old books stored in Mr. Clark's attic, but unfortunately no one was interested enough to record their titles." Other books near at hand are unnoticed by writers on Newton. Francis Trigge (d. 1606), the Puritan clergyman of the neighbouring parish of Welbourn, bequeathed " to the poor of Grantham a valuable collection of books which were kept in a chamber over the south porch of Grantham Church[2]." Trigge was interested in economics as well as theology, and in 1604 published a work, dedicated to the King, against the enclosure of common lands and the conversion of arable land into pasture. Amongst other products of his pen were a volume on the Apocalypse and another on Matthew XIV. An impoverished and omnivorous reader like Newton would not completely neglect the opportunities such a collection afforded for satisfying his taste for theology.

Little is known of Newton's theological studies at Cambridge. Like all contemporary scholars, he was a master of Latin, and used it freely in correspondence. Of his Greek, More remarks[3] : " It is evident that he did not read Greek fluently as all the editions of the Greek fathers (in his library) were in both Greek and Latin." But when Newton wrote, as Sir Herbert Grierson has recently pointed out[4], " Most Greek classics were edited with Latin versions on the opposite page. Even Milton's knowledge of Greek was very limited. In fact the first English poet who was a really scholarly Grecian was Thomas Grey." Newton's Greek has both accents and breathings,

[1] *Ut supra*, p. 14.
[2] *D.N.B. sub voce.*
[3] *Ut supra*, p. 633, n.47.
[4] Presidential Address to English Association, 1948, p. 5.

and his Hebrew the Massoretic points—neither invariably characteristic of Cambridge graduates even in the eighteenth century. It would seem, then, that for his day Newton was well equipped on the philological side to pursue his studies privately in the field of theology. His library, we know, was rich in classical and theological works, especially in the writings of early fathers and Christian historians. It included also works by Socinus and John Crell, and a volume of the *Unitarian Tracts*, promoted by Thomas Firmin (1691), containing works by John Bidle, Stephen Nye and others, prefaced by a life of Bidle.

It has been remarked by Professor Andrade[1] that " nothing is more extraordinary than Newton's development in the period from 1662 to the Spring of 1667," that is, in his early twenties. It may be that he was occupied with theology as well as science during " the leisure and quiet at the little isolated house at Woolstorpe " where he spent most of his time during the great plague from the autumn of 1665 to the spring of 1667, when the University re-opened.

Newton's view of the world may be said to have required him to ponder for himself problems of theology, and settle the terms on which he could stand with regard to the traditional doctrines of God and the Universe. Newton himself, in a memorandum referring to these two years, said : " I was in the prime of my age for invention, and minded mathematics and philosophy more than at any time since." L. T. More observes[2] : " It is altogether probable that ancient history and theology were constantly in his thoughts from youth to extreme age," and Lord Keynes was of opinion[3] that " Very early in life Newton abandoned orthodox belief in the Trinity "—both judgments by men acquainted with his unpublished manuscripts and not obsessed, like Horsley and Brewster, with the desire to conceal the nature of his religious opinions. As early as 1679, eight years before the *Principia* was published, Newton himself, writing to Hooke, said : " But yet my affection to philosophy being worn out . . . I must acknowledge myself averse from spending that time in writing about it which I think I can spend otherwise more to my own content and the good of others." Here he probably had in mind chiefly, if not exclusively, his theological studies.

[1] *Newton Tercentenary Celebrations* (1947) p.4.
[2] *Ut supra*, p. 609.
[3] *Newton Tercentenary Celebrations*, p. 30.

Newton, by his constant refusal to be ordained, risked losing his Fellowship at Trinity, and would have lost it had not Charles II been induced by the Royal Society to issue letters patent in 1675, saying that the holder of the Lucasian Professorship of Mathematics could hold a College Fellowship even if he did not take holy orders, notwithstanding any College statute to the contrary. It is said[1], on the authority of John Conduitt, who married Newton's niece, that Archbishop Tenison offered him, if he would take orders, the Mastership of Trinity College when it was given to Montagu (1683), and importuned him to accept any preferment in the Church, saying to him : " ' Why will you not ? You know more divinity than all of us put together.' ' Why then,' said Newton, ' I shall be able to do you more service then if I was not in orders '."

Newton's opinions are generally described as Arian. Keynes attempted a more precise definition of his theology. " At this time Socinians were an important Arian sect amongst intellectual circles. It may be that Newton fell under Socinian influence, but I think not. He was rather a Judaic monotheist of the school of Maimonides. He arrived at this conclusion, not on so-to-speak rational or sceptical grounds, but entirely on the interpretation of ancient authority. He was persuaded that the revealed documents give no support to the Trinitarian doctrine."

It is a singular statement of truth and error. There is no evidence for the existence of Socinians as " an important Arian sect " at this or any other time. In England, as elsewhere, the essential differences between Arian and Socinian were always recognised, even when, in common opposition to Trinitarianism, they co-operated in more ways than one. It is true, however, that during the last decade of the seventeenth century and the first of the eighteenth, many Arian churchmen, including clergymen, were influenced by Socinian literature from Holland, though the Socinian scheme, as a whole, seems never to have taken root in this country. More[2] classified Anti-Trinitarians as " Arians, Socinians, and Humanitarians or Unitarians," giving the meanings of the first two terms current in the fourth and sixteenth centuries respectively, ignoring the changed connotation of " Socinian " in the eighteenth century, and overlooking the fact that both Arians and Socinians so-called commonly

[1] *Newton Tercentenary Celebrations*, p. 30.
[2] *Ut supra*, p. 630, note 41.

adopted the term " Unitarian " introduced into England from the Netherlands in the preceding century.   It was in print here in 1672 and used by the contributors to the Five Collections of Unitarian Tracts, 1691-1703, including Arians, Socinians and Sabellians, amongst them many episcopalians, both clergymen and laymen. The eight folio volumes of the *Bibliotheca Fratrum Polonorum, Quos Unitarios Vocant*, the storehouse of Socinian scholarship, were published at Amsterdam in 1668. Not a few copies of this massive work and many more portable Socinian books were widely circulated in England before the Toleration Act of 1689. A considerable number of these books were in the library of Locke and some, at least, known to Newton. In the eighteenth century Socinianism was less influential than Arianism until the conversion of Joseph Priestley from Arianism to Socinianism in 1767. Later in the century Arians and Socinians taught in the same nonconformist academies and even occasionally acted as joint-pastors to the same congregation. In England during this century, as Alexander Gordon said : " Socinian was the name given to those who, denying our Lord's pre-existence, assigned him no nature but the human-features of the system of Socinus which in other respects, that of the sonship of Christ and of Christ's present relation to the divine government of the world, had no access to the minds of the so-called Socinians," in other words, they were " Humanitarians or Unitarians."[1]

The most influential Arian publication in episcopal and dissenting circles alike was *The Scripture Doctrine of the Trinity*—a significant title—1st ed. 1712, by Dr. Samuel Clarke, the friend of Newton. A more eccentric advocate of similar doctrine was William Whiston, Clarke's biographer, the quondam friend and successor of Newton in the Cambridge chair which he lost by his outspoken heresy.

Newton, in general an Arian[2], sometimes expressed himself like a Socinian. " Jesus," he said, " by calling himself the Son of God and saying ' I and my Father are one ' meant nothing more than that ' the Father had sanctified him and sent him into the world ' " (John x, 36). The last clause in this sentence may be found word for word in Harnack's summary of the Christology of Socinus[3].

---

[1] For the opinions of Arius and Socinus, see Note on p. 000.
[2] See his discussion of Philippians II, 6, in Common Place Book.
[3] More. *Ut supra*, p. 643 and Harnack, *History of Dogma*, Eng. Trans., VII, 167. In the *Catechism of the Polish Churches*, 1st ed., 1612, published at Stauropolis (Amsterdam), 1680, it is said of Christ : " He alone was sanctified by God and sent into the world."

Samuel Johnson, in his last illness, recommended his physician " to study Dr. Clarke and to read his sermons." On being asked why " he pressed Dr. Clarke, an Arian," he replied : " Because he is fullest on propitiatory sacrifice."

Newton, indeed, speaks of Christ as " sacrificed for us on the cross " and as one who " redeemed us with his blood," but nowhere defines the nature of the Atonement. He describes Jesus as " a true man born of woman, crucified by the Jews for teaching them the truth," but later in the same manuscript[1] identifies him with the great mysterious figures spoken of by Moses, David and the prophets —" Shiloh," "Servant of God," "Lamb of God," "The Holy One," etc., "Who is worshipped and glorified as the Lamb of God . . ." Nevertheless elsewhere[2] he insists at length on the " worship of the One God " by love, trust, prayer, praise . . . , adding, " These things we must do, not to any mediator between him and us, but to him alone." Possibly here he had in mind the worship of saints in the Roman Church.

Polish Socinians rejected the substitutionary theory of Atonement. " Jesus," they said, " was sent by God to men that he might set forth to them the will of God, and might establish agreement with them in his name." Christ's function was essentially prophetic, as Newton frequently represents it. He was certainly acquainted with Socinian literature, for he mentions the Socinians' view of Cyprian in Section IV of " An Historical Account," but acknowledges no indebtedness to them, as he does, for example, to the Arian, Christopher Sand, once in the Treatise named and twice in his MS. note on I John v, 7, 8, in the Common Place Book. The chief contributor to the Unitarian Tracts, Stephen Nye, a clergyman, also pays tribute to Sand in the earliest of them (1st ed., 1687), written at the invitation of Thomas Firmin, an intimate friend of Locke. Newton was for long suspected of having contributed to these Tracts, but, despite marked similarities between their doctrine and his, there is no evidence that he read any of them, nor that the Tract Writers were acquainted with any of the manuscript copies of his discussion of the two texts so frequently adduced as scriptural proofs of the Trinity in the controversies of the time. Amongst Newton's friends in old age was Samuel Crell (1660-1741), member

[1] Our Religion to Christ.
[2] A Short Scheme of True Religion.

of an old Polish Socinian family, who came to England in 1726 to publish a volume on the Proem of John's Gospel. Its purpose was " to demonstrate on the ground of a corrected text of John i, 1, and of the witness of early Fathers, that the chief scriptural foundation of the dogma of the deity of Christ was a corrupt text." Published in two handsome volumes, an edition of 1,000 copies went out of print.[1] In a letter, 17 July, 1726, Crell wrote an account of his visit to Newton, who, we are told, " expressed a wish to read his book, read it when printing," and, " as they parted placed two guineas in his hand for his personal use."[2] This is probably all that can be said of Newton's Socinianism—such as it was.

There is evidence of Newton's interest in Maimonides, whose *Guide for the Perplexed* argued that " God is a free cause, but a rational one, his rationality lying in the homogeneity of his creation." Spinoza was one of his debtors, and Newton, though not a pantheist, may have been another. In his notes from Irenaeus and others, there is one of six pages, " Ex Maimonides de Cultu Divino," and other extracts in a collection of theological notes, whilst in " The Language of the Prophets " he also cites it a few times. For both men laws of Nature are originally divine decrees. Newton was familiar with rabbinical commentaries and with writers like Buxtorf and Lightfoot. The church he regarded as essentially a development of the syagogue. L.T.More[3], summarising his MS. "Irenicum," says : " He argues that the primitive Christian church and its successor the Protestant Church was a continuation of the synagogue and modelled on it. Since, also, a break in the succession occurred in the time of Ezra so an uninterrupted succession of Bishops is not necessary for the being of a Church, as the Roman Church claims." As an exposition of the explicit and implicit meaning of the MS.—so far so good. What follows is astounding. " But his (Newton's) reasoning is defective, because he forgets that the Temple, and the authority of the High Priest grew out of the Synagogue, as the Pope and the Bishop grew out of the Temple." Actually, of course, Temple and High Priest existed and functioned centuries before any synagogue, and the High Priest had nothing to do with the synagogue. When the two existed side by side, they represented two distinct types of worship, and, incidentally, the Temple (until the last few

[1] E. M. Wilbur, *History of Unitarianism* (1945), p. 576.
[2] *Ibid*, note 20.
[3] *Ut supra*, p. 639.

years before its fall) was mainly under the influence of the Sadducees, whilst the synagogue was always the organ of the Pharisees. The Church may have eventually borrowed some of its ritual from the Temple, but the primitive church grew out of the synagogue, and its bishops out of the elders. A chief bishop ultimately became Pope ; his ancestor, however, was not the High Priest, but the Ruler of the Synagogue, who was really little more than what we call " Chairman of Committee."

Newton agreed with Maimonides that " The doors of interpretation are not closed," and, like him, was a moralist and a rationalist, but not a sceptic. Maimonides, however, aimed at a reconciliation of Aristotelian philosophy with Jewish theology, whilst Newton, in [his own words[1], held " That religion and philosophy are to be preserved distinct. We are not to introduce divine revelations into philosophy nor philosophical opinions into religion."

Newton's rationalism is apparent in doctrinal, biblical, and historical writings, though not equally in all.

" Homoousion," he said, " is unintelligible. 'Twas not understood in the Council of Nice, nor ever since. What cannot be understood is no object of belief."

The Creeds are no part of revealed religion ; hence, with the exception of what he termed " the so-called Apostles Creed," whose phraseology is scriptural, and says nothing of the Trinity, Incarnation, Deity of Christ or personality of the Holy Spirit, there was for Newton no curb to the exercise of reason in relation to 'them. Theophilus Lindsey, when he turned Unitarian, retained the Apostles Creed in the first edition of his Prayer Book. Again, in the " sentence " which introduces the entries in Newton's Common Place Book, we read : " A man may imagine things that are false, but he can only understand things that are true, for if the things be false the apprehension of them is not understanding." In this connection his brief note on miracle is important. " For miracles are so called not because they are the works of God, but because they happen seldom, and for that reason create wonder. If they should happen constantly according to certain laws impressed upon the nature of things, they would be no longer wonders or miracles, but might be considered in philosophy as a part of the phenomena of nature (notwithstanding their being the effects of the laws impressed

---

[1] MS. " Seven Statements of Religion."

upon nature by the powers of God) notwithstanding that the cause of their causes might be unknown to us." More, in a footnote, calls attention to the fact that " the passage in brackets was written and then crossed (out)." It seems consonant with Newton's theory of the operations of deity, but probably on second thoughts the following alternative sentence was preferred to it. In any event Newton's views of miracle is not orthodox.

In his bulky manuscript on " The Language of the Prophets " he acknowledges his debt to Henry More, but by " Language " he means not the simple vocabulary but its significance on a comparative study of different " prophets," who " all wrote in one and the same mystical language." In the main it is an attempt to elucidate the Book of Revelation in relation to the history of East and West, not without trenchant criticism of Roman Catholic developments in doctrine and discipline. In his posthumously published book on Daniel, Newton does not question the veracity of Daniel, and declares that to reject its prophecies " is to reject the Christian religion. For this religion is founded upon his Prophecy concerning the Messiah." Newton shared with Locke his doctrine of the Messiahship of Jesus as central to Christianity, and with Priestley his singular devotion to the dreams of Daniel. In a letter, "Feb. 7, 1690-1," to Locke, who, referring to Daniel VII, had said that " the Ancient of Days " is Christ, Newton, then engaged on the book published six years after his death, asked : " Whence are you certain that the Ancient of Days is Christ ? Does Christ anywhere sit upon the throne ? " In a later letter, 30 June, 1691, he referred again to these questions. " There seems to be a mistake either in my last letter, or in yours, because you write in your former letter, that the Ancient of Days is Christ ; and in my last, I either did, or should have asked, how you knew that. But these discourses may be done with more freedom at our next meeting." The questions show that Newton held firmly the doctrine of the supremacy of the Father, not, as More supposed, that " at this time Newton was sceptical of Daniel's prophecy as predicting the coming of Christ."

The editor of the *Catalogue of the Newton MSS.* (1936) observes : " The Alchemy that Newton practised had more than its vocabulary in common with Mysticism, and no doubt it was by way of Alchemy that Newton entered upon the interpretation of Prophecies which form so large a part of his Theological writings."

It is for those familiar with the language of Newton in his MSS. on Alchemy to say how far their phraseology pertains to the vocabulary of Mysticism. Professor Andrade assures us that " his library was well stocked with the standard alchemical and mystical books," wherein " allegory tinged with prophecy, coloured with religious belief, and clouded with charlatanism " may be found. Mysticism, as we understand it, has a richer, deeper, and more fundamentally religious content than is suggested by this description of Newton's books. There is some doubt, however, about Alchemy being " the way by which he entered upon the interpretation of prophecy." Neither published nor unpublished writings, so far as examined, seem to support this conclusion. His work on Prophecy is largely, though not exclusively, built up on material drawn from Scripture, and its symbols derive in the main from the same source, though vitally affected by his theory of hermeneutics. Reasoning is restrained by an inspired authority and motived by the belief, shared with the first evangelist, that prophecy pointed to Jesus as Messiah from birth to death. It may be said of Newton, scientific genius as he was, that in his study of Prophecy he yielded to the temptation, present to early Greek thinkers, to trace the action and method of divine government without a sufficient basis of facts. It could hardly be otherwise in the infancy of scientific historical study and biblical criticism. None the less, within the limits stated, he implicitly accepted, with Locke and Priestley, the principle of the authority of scripture interpreted by reason. Locke's more sober discussions of the Pauline epistles passed through his hands, and Daniel, as we have seen, was one of the subjects of their correspondence. The principle aforesaid, inherited from Locke, prevailed with Unitarian scholars until the middle of the last century. Newton's rationalism, however defective, must be given due recognition. Outside Prophecy he found more scope for its exercise. Occasionally anti-Romanism blended with rationalism to produce quaint biblical exegesis. Thus we find an allusion to the Petrine claims (based on Matt. xvi, 15), when after speaking of " the gates in the cities of Israel where laws were administered, and sometimes on a neighbouring hill there was a high place for sacrifice," he adds, " And in this sense it is said that the gates of hell, that is, the magistrates in the gates of idolatrous cities, shall not prevail against the true Church of God."[1]

In a letter to Thomas Burnet, January, 1680-1, on his *Telluris*

[1] " Irenicum," Thesis 1.

Theoria Sacra (1681), Newton, answering a request for his opinion of it, rejects the literal interpretation of the Genesis account of creation, and said *inter alia* : " As to Moses, I do not think his description of the creation either philosophical or feigned, but that he describes realities in a language artificially adapted to the sense of the vulgar." In Section XXXVI of " An Historical Account " he remarks : " If it be said we are not to determine what is Scripture, and what not, by our private judgments, I confess it in places, not controverted ; but in disputable places, I love to take up with what I understand . . . . I have that honour for him (St. John) as to believe that he wrote good sense ; and therefore take that sense to be *his* which is the best." Of the Nicene and Athanasian Creeds he says in one MS. : "They are indeed appointed by the Common Prayer Book to be read in the Churches upon certain occasions.   And so are many parts of the Scripture which we do not understand.   We daily dispute about the meaning of these, and so we may about the meaning of the two Creeds."   Like the contemporary Unitarian writers, Newton takes his stand on the 8th Article of the Church that " the three Creeds are to be received because they may be proved by most certain warrant of Scripture. . . . Therefore are we authorised by the Church to compare them with the Scriptures and see how and in what sense they can be deduced thereform.   And when we cannot see the Deduction, we are not to rely upon the authority of Councils or Synods. . . . The 6th Article declares that the Holy Scripture contains all things necessary to salvation ; so that whatsoever is not read therein, nor may be proved thereby, is not to be required of any man that it should be believed. . . ."[1]

Many twentieth century writers on Newton have stressed the influence of Jacob Boehme upon his theological and scientific thought, a tradition going back to William Law (1686-1761). Stephen Hobhouse has named nine such writers.   Professor Andrade is the tenth.   Writing in 1946, he said[2] : " Newton was a close student of Jacob Boehme, from whose works he copied large extracts." It may be so, but there appears to be little trace of them, and none of Boehme's works were found in Newton's library at the time of his death.   Earlier writers went further and accepted Law's statement[3], quoted by Christopher Walton that "Sir Isaac did but reduce to a

[1] MS. "Irenicon."
[2] *Newton Tercentenary Celebrations*, p. 20.
[3] *Memorials of William Law* (1854), p. 84.

mathematical form the central principles of nature revealed in Behmen." Hobhouse has recently investigated the origin of the tradition and finally disposed of its veracity. He proved that Law's oral authority for it was untrustworthy ; that the scientist did not derive from the mystic his doctrine of the attractive force of gravity and other principles of physics ; and that Newton knew little, if anything, of Boehme with whom he had nothing in common. In a volume published in 1948, after an analysis of Boehme's thought, he writes :[1]

> We have here a subtle union of pantheism and dualism of which Newton probably had not the remotest understanding. His system knows nothing of pantheism, and his dualism is of a totally different kind. . . . To Newton, the transcendent personal God with His spiritual counterpart man, stands on one side, and on the other the mechanical system of matter, motion, and force, into which no spiritual essence, no strife of good and evil intrudes. Newton has apparently no conception even of the need of a theory of knowledge to bridge the gulf between God and His world. His hypothetical aether as the possible medium of God's percipience and activity is a crude mechanical device which could satisfy no metaphysician. This is far removed from a mysticism such as that of Boehme. Newton was a diligent student of the Bible and a conforming, though unorthodox Churchman. . . . He certainly had a profound reverence for the operations of God in nature, and probably too for His operations in the human soul. But he kept his religion apart from his philosophy, and appears to have made no attempt to reconcile the two.

In a footnote we are informed that after " considerable correspondence and conversation with him," Professor More allowed Hobhouse " to state that he has altered his view expressed in his biography as to the influence of Boehme upon Newton."

Newton's MSS. confirm Hobhouse's views of his teaching, his resolve to treat philosophy and religion as two separate spheres, and the absence of reference to Boehme and his mysticism. There is no call to qualify Hobhouse's statement respecting Newton's philosophy, but something more may be said of his religion.

[1] *Selected Mystical Writings of William Law*, 2nd ed., revised (1948), pp. 397-422.

Professor C. C. J. Webb has said[1] that " reason and conscience are considered (by theists) as the ' image ' of reality (God), which is manifested in all phenomena but reveals itself in the evocation from the human spirit of the sentiment of reverence, which belongs to the essence of religion, and culminates in the love of God ' with all the heart and soul and mind and strength ' prescribed by the first of the two great commandments of the Christian gospel."   Newton held no such conception of conscience as Butler and Martineau, and no doctrine of incarnation like that of the latter who declared " The Incarnation is true, not of Christ exclusively, but of Man universally. . . The spiritual light in us which forms our higher spiritual life is of one substance (homoousion) with his own righteousness "—a doctrine closely related to that of the Quakers.   Yet the scientist was animated by the reverence which " culminates in the love of God," and felt the need of man " to love his neighbour as himself," which together witness to Newton's belief in man's capacity for fellowship, human and divine.   Incidentally, it may be noted that the two commandments, one from Deuteronomy and the other from Leviticus, were first combined (three times) in the " Testaments of the Twelve Patriarchs," dated by R. H. Charles, 109-10 B.C., and therefore not primarily " of the Christian gospel," though stated there more emphatically and vigorously than elsewhere.   Nothing in Newton's MSS. is more strongly or frequently emphasised than these commandments.   They occur in six different drafts of the " Irenicum " ; twice in " A Short Scheme of Religion," and several times elsewhere, besides many allusions to their contents. He traces the religion of loving God and neighbour throughout the history of the Hebrews, and characterizes it as " also the principal part of the religion of the Christians."   Here it may be pertinent to note that when speaking[2] of the last judgment in the language of gospel, epistle and apocalypse, Newton says nothing of hell or eternal torments, but avoiding the word Purgatory, states that " Christ sent the wicked to places suitable to their merits."   This is no mere euphemism, for another version includes the " places " amongst the " many mansions " in which the blessed have their abode ; doctrine, be it observed, more Catholic than Protestant.   Whiston, in early religious meditations (1686) accepted the common view of eternal torments, but altered his opinion, justified it (1717), and in his

[1] *Religion and Theism*, pp. 125-126.
[2] Our Religion to Christ.

Life of Samuel Clarke (1743) said : " I may venture to add, upon the credit of what I have discovered of the opinions of Sir Isaac Newton and Dr. Clarke, that few or no thinking men were really of different sentiments in that matter."

In discussions of religion, Newton ranges far beyond the confines of Judaism and Christianity. Writing " Of Humanity," he cites laws " acknowledged by Heathens, taught by Socrates, Confucius, and other philosophers ; the Israelites by Moses and the prophets, and the Christians more fully by Christ and his Apostles. This is that law which the Apostle tells you was written on the hearts of the Gentiles, Rom. ii, 13-16. . . Thus you see there is but one law for all nations, the law of righteousness and charity, dictated to the Christians by Christ, to the Jews by Moses, to all mankind by the light of reason."

In such a context " reason " is not far removed from " conscience," and the identification of its pronouncements with the righteousness of the lawgiver and the love of Christ is an evidence of the breadth and depth of Newton's religion.

Newton's zeal for Protestantism against Romanism is undoubted. Professor A. D. Ritchie, lecturing in 1943 on " Sir Isaac Newton : The Man and his Influence[1] " said not only that " The main purpose of his theological studies was to uphold Protestantism and refute the claims of the Roman Church" ; but also that " The historical study of the doctrine of the Trinity was made for this purpose." Many of Newton's notes on doctrine, however, have no specific reference to Roman Catholicism, and others are philosophical or historical in character. Fourteen " Argumenta " in Latin seek to prove that the Son is not co-eternal with, nor equal to the Father, and are based on scriptural proofs. What Professor Ritchie called " More's careful and well-documented biography " quotes six of these arguments. Of course orthodox Protestants not less than Romanists would challenge the exegesis of the texts cited. Another manuscript gives seven " Rationes " against the Trinity, which are mainly philosophical. More quoted three, of which that on " Homoousion " has already been noticed. No. 6 runs : " The Father is God, creating and a person ; the Son is God, created and a person ; and the Holy Ghost is God, proceeding and a person : ' et tamen non est

---

[1] Memoirs of Manchester Literary and Philosophical Society, Vol. 85, p. 5. Reprinted in *Essays in Philosophy* (1948), p. 170.

nisi unus Deus '." This is followed by an illustration. " There is a Western Church, an Oriental Church, and an Egyptian Church, *et tamen non est nisi unus Ecclesia.*" No. 7, " The Person is intellectual substance (substantia intellectualis), therefore the three Persons are three substances." The manuscripts entitled " Para-doxical Questions concerning the Morals and Actions of Athanasius and his Followers " and " Twenty-two Queries regarding the word ' Homoousion ' " are historical and philosophical respectively. The doctrine of the Trinity in one form or another has always been accepted by orthodox Protestants, and in " An Historical Account of Two Notable Corruptions of Scripture " Beza the reformer is handled not less severely than earlier Roman Catholic scholars for his treatment of the texts discussed. In the opening paragraph of this Treatise, Newton, writing to Locke, refers to the current con-troversy in the Church of England. " Since the discourses of some late writers have raised in you a curiosity of knowing the truth of that text of Scripture concerning the testimony of the Three in Heaven, I John v, 7, I have sent you an account of what the reading has been in all ages and by what steps it has been changed, so far as I can hitherto determine by records." In 1689 appeared Father Richard Simon's *Histoire critique du texte du Nouveau Testament,* and in the following year his *Histoire critique des versions du Nouveau Testament.* In 1690, the year Newton sent Locke the Treatise, were published *The Naked Gospel,* by Arthur Bury ; *The Doctrine of the Trinity,* by John Wallis ; a reply to the last-named by William Sherlock, entitled *A Vindication of the Holy and Ever-Blessed Trinity ;* and *A Vindication of the Unitarians,* Anon, by William Freke. Neither in the Trinitarian controversy of Anglican divines nor in the Unitarian Tracts it evoked is there any indication that the Trinity was a subject dividing Protestant from Catholic, and all the controversialists, Trinitarian and Unitarian, discuss conceptions of it current in the established church. If Newton's attacks upon texts interpolated in the New Testament were necessarily and therefore primarily directed against Church Fathers, they were not less effective against Protestants who defended the *Textus Receptus.* Beza, for example, said of the second disputed text, I Timothy iii, 16 : " There is scarcely another passage in which all the mysteries of our redemption are explained so magnificently or so clearly." Newton, speaking of this text, makes another allusion to the controversy then raging, " In all the times of the hot and lasting Arian controversy, it never came into play, though now these disputes are over, they that read ' God manifest in the flesh ' think it one of the most obvious and pertinent texts for the business." Again, when Newton, in the Treatise, speaks of the baptismal formula in Matthew xxviii, 19, as " the place from which they tried at first to derive the Trinity "—an expression that offended Horsley—the word " they " suggests orthodox Christians with whom he had no sympathy, and the word " tried " implies that the attempt proved unsuccessful. Newton used the formula in his manuscripts, as did English Unitarians in liturgies and baptismal services generally until the end of the nineteenth century.

It is most probable that Newton's attention was directed to the texts which constituted the main biblical supports for the doctrine of the Trinity when, on the evidence of Scripture generally as on philosophical grounds, he had rejected the doctrine of the Trinity, and it is certain that his study of the doctrine was not made for the purpose simply of upholding Protestantism against Roman Catholicism.

Now, more than two centuries after his death, the results of Newton's prolonged labours in the field of theology have been fully brought to light, and it does not appear, as Professor Ritchie supposed, that in these studies " Newton was entirely a child of the period."

NOTE ON ARIUS AND SOCINUS.

Arius and Socinus were agreed on the central doctrine of Unitarianism—the recognition of a single personality in the godhead, but differed fundamentally in their conceptions of the person and work of Christ. For Arius Christ was a creation *sui generis* and not of the same substance as the Father. He was the divine agent in creation ; became the incarnate logos, and, though not possessed of a human soul, suffered for our salvation. Socinus regarded him as essentially man, who, at the beginning of his ministry, was carried up into heaven (an interpretation of Johannine passages) and received a unique revelation of divine truth, He was Saviour as publisher of salvation, reconciling man to God (not God to man), and as our example. Above all he was the divine ambassador and prophet. After death, he was endowed with an official deity, in virtue of which adoration of him was imperative and direct address in prayer permissive, whilst as mediator prayer to the Father was through him. Francis David, the contemporary of Socinus, renounced the worship of Christ, and founded the existing Hungarian Unitarian Church.

c

IRENICUM

PREFACE

Of the seven drafts of " Irenicum " four bear the title, but only one has the addition " Or Ecclesiastical Polity Tending To Peace." Two drafts are divided into sections, one of which has 9 " Positions " and the other, 20 " Theses."

It appears on internal evidence that the order in which the several parts are here given may well be that of their composition. The last alone has hitherto been printed.   See Brewster's *Memoirs of Sir Isaac Newton*, Vol. II, Appendix, No. XXVII.

These writings on Christian Doctrine, Church Government, Relations of Church and State, and the conditions governing membership of the church, though brief, constitute one of the most important of the Newton theological manuscripts.   Its purpose is, apparently, to promote Comprehension in the established church and set forth a *modus vivendi* for English Protestants.

[IRENICUM]

The First Position

In the religion of the Jews the two first and great commandments were " Thou shalt love the Lord thy God with all thy heart and with all thy soul and with all thy mind and thou shalt love thy neighbour as thyself. Upon these two commandments hang all the Law and the Prophets." Matt. xxii, 37.

The Second Position

The religion of loving God and our neighbour was the religion of Noah and his sons down to the days of Abraham, Melchisedek, Job and Moses. For Noah was a just man, very righteous and perfect in his generation and walked with God (Gen. vi, 9 ; Ezek. xiv, 14). Melchisedek had his name from justice and righteousness, and was a priest of the most high God, and acknowledged such by Abraham, who paid tithes to him and was blessed by him, and Christ himself was a Priest after the order of Melchisedek, not after the order of Aaron, but after the order of the Patriarchs (Gen. xiv ; Hebs. vii). And Job feared God and eschewed evil, and tells us that to worship the Sun or Moon was to forsake the God above and to commit an evil punishable in his country by the judge. He condemned also deceit, adultery, uncharitableness, covetousness, pride and rejoicing at the misfortunes of enemies, as crimes in his country. While mankind lived together in Chaldea under the government of Noah, they were all of his religion, and in the days of Peleg when they divided the earth they carried this religion along with them and kept it for a while.

The Third Position

The loving God and neighbour is also the principal part of the religion of Christians. For this is the love of God that we keep his commandments, and the love of neighbour is that charity without which no man can be saved. 1 John v, 3 ; 1 Cor. xiii, Rom. xiii, 8-10 ; Jas. ii, 8. This commandment have we from him that he who loveth God love his brother also, 1 John iv, 21.

The Fourth Position

In the primitive Church all things necessary to the remission of sins and salvation were taught in catechising in order to baptism. For baptism was unto the remission of sins, and he whose sins are remitted is in a state of salvation. I do not say that sins are remitted by baptism. They are remitted by a sincere repentance from dead works (such are the lust of the flesh, the lust of the eye, and the pride of life, and the worship of Demons or Ghosts) and by a sincere belief in what was taught in the primitive Creeds. And Baptism was only a sign or symbol of the remission of sins by the washing away of the filth of the body.

The Fifth Position

In the primitive Church it was not lawful to impose any other article of religion as necessary to the remission of sins and salvation besides those which were taught from the beginning of the Gospel in catechising. For when some Christians of the circumcision would have imposed circumcision upon the Gentiles saying that unless they were circumcised they could not be saved, Acts xv, 1, the Apostle Paul in opposition to them tells the Galatians, " If we or an Angel from heaven preach any other Gospel than that which we have preached unto you, let him be accursed," Gal. i, 8. It was lawful for the Christians of the circumcision to circumcise their own children ; and the Apostle circumcised Timothy because his mother was a Jew, Acts xvi, 1, 3. The Gentiles had revolted from the religion of Noah to worship false gods. And now by the preaching of the Gospel, returned not to the religion of Moses but to that of their ancestors from which they had revolted. And therefore they were to abstain from the blood of animals. For this religion obliged men to be merciful even to brute beasts.

The Sixth Position

If any man of this religion have been either false Prophets or otherwise wicked ; it will not follow from thence that the religion itself is either false or wicked.

The Seventh Position

In the first year of the reign of Darius the Mede over Chaldea, the Angel Gabriel appeared to Daniel and said to him, " Seventy weeks are determined upon thy people and upon thy holy city to finish the transgression, and to make an end of sins, and to make reconciliation for iniquity, and to bring in everlasting righteousness, and to seal up the vision and prophecy, and to anoint the most Holy." Daniel ix, 24. And the ancient Jews interpreted these weeks to be such as the work of Laban and Jacob (Gen. xxix, 27), that is weeks of years, for they expected the Messiah in the days of Augustus Caesar or soon after, that is, at the end of seventy such weeks or 490 years, and put their trust into such an expectation. And some took Herod for the Messiah and were thence called Herodians, others took Thendas for the Messiah, and others Judas of Galilee. And this expectation continued until the days of Hadrian when Barchochba, another false Messiah, was slain.

The Eighth Position

By the Babylonians captivity the government of the Jews was dissolved and they ceased to be a body politic for a time and became again a people, and Jerusalem, their holy city from the time that Ezra by the commission of Artaxerxes Longimanus reunited them into a body politic by setting up magistrates and Judges to govern and teach the people in Judea and punish offenders against the laws of God and the king unto death and banishment or confiscation of goods or imprisonment. And from that time to the death of Jesus Christ were just 70 weeks or 490 years. And because the most holy was to be anointed at the end of the days, thence Jesus was called the Messiah and the Christ, that is, the anointed, and thence his followers were called Christians.

The Ninth Position

In the second Psalm are these words, " Thou art my son, this day have I begotten thee. Ask of me and I shall give thee the heathen for thine inheritance and the utmost parts of the earth for thy possession. Thou shalt break them with a rod of iron and shalt dash them in pieces like a potter's vessel." And these words the Apostles and primitive Christians applied to Jesus Christ as being the son of God by the resurrection from the dead, and being to come again in the end of ages, and rule all nations with a rod of iron. Acts xiii, 37 ; Rom. i, 4.

[Unfinished]

[IRENICUM]

And the gospel is that Jesus is the Christ. " Whosoever believeth that Jesus is the Christ is born of God : and every one that loveth him that begat loveth him also that is begotten of him." 1 John v, i. See also Luke xxiv, 21-27 ; 44-47 ; Matthew xxviii, 18-20 ; Luke xxiv, 49, 50. And all this is the Gospel which Christ sent his disciples to teach all nations and which the first Christians were taught in catechising before baptism and communion.

Repentance and remission of sins relate to transgressions against the two first commandments. We are to forsake the Devil, that is, all false gods and all manner of idolatry, this being a breach of the first and great commandment. And we are to forsake the flesh and the world, or as the Apostle John expressed it, the lust of the flesh and the lust of the eye and the pride of life, that is unchastity, covetousness, pride and ambition ; these things being a breach of the second of the two great commandments. And we are to believe in one God, the father, almighty in dominion, the maker of heaven and earth and of all things therein, and in our Lord Jesus Christ, the son of God, who was born of a Virgin and sacrificed for us on the cross, and the third day rose again from the dead and ascended unto heaven, and sitteth on the right hand of God in a mystical sense, being next unto him in honour and power, who shall come again to judge the quick and the dead raised to life, and who sent the Holy Ghost to comfort his disciples and assist them in preaching the Gospel.

All this was taught from the beginning of the Gospel in catechising, that the Catechumens might know before Baptism why and in whose names he was to be washed, viz. in the name of one God the Father and of our Lord Jesus Christ.

And nothing more is now necessary to communion and salvation than what was taught in those days before baptism and admission into communion. For everything necessary to communion must be taught before admission into it.

All this the Apostle Paul calls milk for babes and the foundation and first principles of the doctrine of Christ. And those things which are to be learnt after admission into Communion he calls strong meat for men of riper years. For in writing to the Hebrews, he saith, " When for the time ye ought to be teachers, ye have need that one teach you again which be the first principles of the oracles of God ; and are become such as have need of milk and not of strong meat. . . . Therefore leaving the principles of the doctrine of Christ, let us go on unto perfection ; not laying again the foundation of repentance from dead works, and of faith toward God, and of the doctrine of baptisms, and of laying on of hands, and of the resurrection of the dead, and of eternal judgment." Heb. v, 12-14 ; vi, 1-2.

Here the Apostle, under the name of milk for babes, comprehends all that was taught before baptism and admission into communion, and, under the name of strong meat, comprehends all that was to be learnt afterwards by men of riper years by studying the scriptures or otherwise. And since strong meats are not fit for babes, but are to be given only to men of riper years, they were not to be imposed on all men, but only to be learnt by such as after admission into communion were able to learn them.

And by consequence men were not to damn or excommunicate one another, or hate or despise or censure one another for not knowing them. Every man after communion was to study the scriptures and especially the Prophecies, and to learn as much as he could out of them, and might endeavour to instruct his neighbour in a friendly manner, but not fall out with him for differences of opinion about anything which was not imposed before baptism and admission into communion. For enmity and discord in things not necessary to communion tends to schisms, and is contrary to the rule of charity imposed upon all men, and very especially upon those of the same community, in the second of the two first commandments. " And with what judgment ye judge ye shall be judged." See Rom. xiv, xvi and I Cor. xiii.

If anything at any time be made necessary to communion which was not so before, it ought thenceforward to be taught before admission into communion.

And as for the Christian worship, we are authorized in scripture to give glory and honour to God the father, because he hath created all things, and to the Lamb of God, because he hath redeemed us with his blood and is our Lord, and to direct our prayers to God the father in the name of Christ for what we want, and give him thanks for what we receive, and to wish for grace and peace from God and Christ and the Holy Ghost, and baptise in their name, and to receive the Eucharist in memory of Christ's death. And this was practised by the first Christians in the Apostles' days from the time of their admission into Communion, and is included in the first principles of the doctrine of Christ ; and if any man contend for any other sort of worship which he cannot prove to have been practised in the Apostles' days, he may use it in his Closet without troubling the Churches with his private sentiments. And since Christ set on foot the Christian religion by explaining to his Apostles the prophecies in Moses, the Prophets and the Psalms concerning himself, and sending them to teach his interpretations to all nations ; if any question at any time arise concerning his interpretations, we are to have recourse to the Old Testament and compare the places interpreted with the interpretations of the New. As, for instance, in explaining why Jesus is called the Christ[1] or Messiah, the Son of Man,[2] the Son of God,[3] the Lamb of God,[4] the Word of God[5] and the Lord who sitteth on

[1] Dan. ix, 24, 25.　[2] Dan. vii, 13.　[3] Ps. ii, 7-9.　[4] Exod. xii, 21-23, 27, 46; xxix, 38.
[5] Isa. xi, 4.

the right hand of God, the God[1] who was in the beginning with God and by whom all things were made. And by this means the Old Testament will be also better understood. So then for these names of Christ we are to have recourse to the Old Testament, and to beware of vain Philosophy, for Christ sent his Apostles not to teach Philosophy to the common people and to their wives and children, but to teach what he had taught, taken out of Moses and the Prophets and Psalms concerning Christ.

And as the prophecies of the Old Testament remained in obscurity till Christ's first coming and then were interpreted by Christ, and the interpretations became the religion of the Christians ; so the prophecies of both Testaments relating to Christ's second coming may remain in obscurity till that coming, and then be interpreted by divine authority and the interpretations become the religion of God's people till Christ has put all things under his feet in heaven and earth, and shall deliver up the kingdom to the father. And therefore it is no objection against the Christian religion that the prophecies which relate to Christ's second coming remain still in obscurity.

The first principles of the Christian religion are founded, not on disputable conclusions, or human sanctions, opinions, or conjectures, but on the express words of Christ and his Apostles, and we are to hold fast the form of sound words of scripture. It is not enough that a Proposition be true or in the express words of scripture. It must also appear to have been taught from the days of the Apostles in order to baptism and communion, for baptism into the remission of sin is of divine institution, and laws of God are unalterable by men. It is the character of his people that they keep his commandments, 1 John ii, 3-4 ; v, 2-3 ; Apoc. xii, 17, and that of their enemies that they change times and seasons (Dan. vii, 25). Temporal laws may be made by men about the changeable circumstances of religion, and temporal judges may be appointed to put the laws of both God and the King in execution (Ezra vii, 25-26). But the Gospel which Christ sent his Apostles to preach is not

[1] Gen. ii, 16, 17; iii, 8-11; iv, 6, 9; xviii, 1, 17, 21; xix, 24; Exod, xix, 18; xxiii, 21, 22, etc.

alterable by human authority. It is as much the law of God as the Law of Moses was, and as unalterable. The High Priest and the Sanhedrim itself had no power to alter the law of Moses, and if an Angel from heaven preach any other Gospel than that which the Apostles preached (imposing it as a law of God necessary to baptism, communion and salvation) let him be accursed. (Gal. i, 8, 9).

Idolatry is a breach of the first and greatest commandment. It is giving to idols the love, honour and worship which is due to the true God alone. It is forsaking the true God to commit whoredom with other lovers. It makes a Church guilty of apostasy from God, as an adulteress forsakes her husband. It makes her become the Church of the idols, false gods or Demons whom she worships, such a Church as in Scripture is called a Synagogue of Satan. The Apostle Paul opposed the preaching of the law of Moses to the Gentiles and called it another gospel whereby the faith in Christ was made void, not because the Law was evil (for the Apostle tells us that the Law is good) but because it was not necessary to salvation, and therefore not to be imposed as a fundamental article of communion. And for the same reason the imposing of any Proposition (true or false) as an Article of Communion, which was not an Article of Communion from the first preaching of the Gospel may be preaching another Gospel ; and the persecuting of any true Christians for not receiving that Gospel may be persecuting Christ in his mystical members, and the Persecutor breaks the second and third great commandments in making war upon Christ, and may deserve the name of an Anti-Christian in a literal sense.

A Church guilty of this crime is in a state of apostasy from Christ.

[THE CHURCH OF ENGLAND, THE CREEDS AND ARTICLES]

The fundamental requisites to communion in the Church of England are :

1.   To renounce the Devil and all his works, the vain pomps and glory of the world with all the covetous designs of the same, and the carnal desires of the flesh, so as not to follow nor be led by them, that is, to renounce idolatry, ambition, pride, covetousness and unchastity.   And this the Apostle calls repentance from dead works.

2.   To profess the faith contained in the Creed usually called The Apostles Creed.   And the profession of faith in the primitive Church the Apostle calls faith towards God and the resurrection of the dead and eternal judgment.

3.   To keep the commandments, that is the ten commandments as is explained in the Church Calendar. These and baptism and laying on of hands are all the fundamental requisites to communion in the Church of England.   And therefore to excommunicate any man for anything else is contrary to the fundamental constitution of this Church.   It is to excommunicate a man who, according to the fundamental constitution and express declaration of this Church, became by baptism and laying on of hands a member of Christ, a child of God, and an inheritor of the kingdom of heaven, and may be still so as much as he was at his admission into communion for anything objected against him.

The Constantinopolitan Creed, usually called the Nicene Creed and the Creed usually called the Creed of Athanasius are not therefore any part of the milk for babes in the Church of England, but are to be referred to the strong meats for them that are of ripe age ; and therefore to fall out about them proceeds from the want of Charity.   They are indeed appointed by the Common Prayer Book to be read in the Churches upon certain occasions.   And so are many parts of the Scriptures which we do not understand, as Dan. ix, x ; Apoc. iv, vii, xii,

7-13 ; xiv, 6, 19 ; 1-17. We daily dispute about the meaning of these and many other parts of Scripture without falling out about them, and are allowed to do so. And so we may about the meaning of the two Creeds, notwithstanding their being read in Churches.

The Church of England in her 21st Article declared that General Councils (forasmuch as they be an Assembly of men whereof all be not governed with the spirit and word of God) may err and sometimes have erred in things pertaining to God : and therefore things ordained by them as necessary to salvation have neither strength nor authority, unless it be declared that they are taken out of the holy Scripture. And in the 8th Article she declares that the three Creeds are to be received because they may be proved by most certain warrants of holy Scripture. She doth not require us to receive them by authority of General Councils, and much less by authority of Convocations, but only because they are taken out of the Scriptures. And therefore are we authorised by the Church to compare them with the Scriptures, and see how and in what sense they can be deduced from thence. And when we cannot see the Deduction we are not to rely upon the Authority of Councils and Synods, but may endeavour to learn from others how they may be deduced, and that others are not to fall out with us for doing so.

The Council of Ephesus, which was one of the four General Councils, ordained that nothing should be added to the Constantinopolitan Creed, now commonly called the Nicene. And yet the Latins had added the "filioque" to this Creed, and the Church of England has ordered the Creed with the addition to be read in Churches, contrary to the Decree of one of the four General Councils. And other things which are not in the Constantinopolitan Creed are added to the Creed usually attributed to Athanasius, contrary to the said Decree of the Council of Ephesus. The Church of England therefore lays no stress upon General Councils, but grounds all her religion upon the Scripture.

The Church of England in her 6th Article declares that the " Holy Scripture contains all things necessary to salvation : so that whatsoever is not read therein, nor may be proved thereby, is not to be required of any man, that it should be believed as an Article of Faith, or be thought requisite or necessary to salvation." And in her 8th Article she saith only of the three Creeds that they " ought thoroughly to be received " because " they may be proved by certain warrants of holy Scripture." 'Tis not upon the authority of General Councils, not upon authority of Convocations, or any Church authority, but upon that of the holy Scripture that she recommends them to be received. And in her 20th Article— that the Churches, as those of Jerusalem, Alexandria, Antioch and Rome, etc., and even General Councils have erred and may err in matters of faith, and what they decree as necessary to salvation is of no strength or authority unless they can be shown to be taken from the holy Scripture.

IRENICUM : OR ECCLESIASTICAL POLITY
TENDING TO PEACE

Thesis 1

The cities of the Israel before the Babylonian captivity were governed by elders, who sat in the gate of the city, and put the laws of Moses in execution, and had a place of worship in or near the gate, and sometimes a high place for sacrificing upon a neighbouring hill. See Deut. xix, 12, and xxi, 19, 20, 21, and xxii, 18, 19, and xxv, 7, 8, and Ruth iv, 2, and Josh. xx, 4, and Psal. vii, 4-8. And in this sense it is said that the gates of hell, that is the magistrates in the gates of idolatrous cities, shall not prevail against the true Church of Christ.

Thesis 2

The government of the Jewish Church, being dissolved by the Babylonian captivity, was restored by the commission of Artaxerxes Longimanus, King of Persia, to Ezra, authorizing him to set magistrates and judges to judge the people who knew the laws of God, and to teach them who knew them not, and to execute judgment upon those who would not do the Law of God and the law of the King, whether it were unto death or to banishment, or to confiscation of goods or to imprisonment.

For the forming of this government being left to the discretion of Ezra, it may be presumed that he would pursue the ancient form of Jewish government as far as it was practicable. See Ezra x, 14.

Thesis 3

The government then set up by Ezra was by courts of judicature composed of elders ; the highest court being the Sanhedrim, composed of 70 elders, originally instituted by Moses ; and the second court being composed of 23 elders in the outward gate of the temple ; and the other courts sitting in the synagogues of the cities, and being composed of the elders of the city, not more in number than 23, not fewer than three (see Matt. x, 17, and xxiii, 34 ; Luke xii, 11, and xxi, 12).

Thesis 4

The government set up by Ezra continued till the days of Christ, and was then extended over all the Roman Empire ; and the Jews, by the permission or connivance of the Romans, erected synagogues wherever they were sufficiently numerous to do it ; and the elders of cities were called rulers of their synagogues (see Acts xv, 21 ; Matt. x, 17 and xxiii, 34, and Luke xii, 11, and xxi, 12).

Thesis 5

The same government continued among the converted Jews of the circumcision in the regions of Phoenicia, Syria, etc., till the end of the fourth century, or longer, and the chief ruler of the synagogue was called by them the Prince of the Synagogue.

Thesis 6

The same government was propagated from the Jews to the converted Gentiles, the name of synagogues being changed to that of churches, and the name of Chief Rulers and Princes of the Synagogues into that of Presidents and Bishops, the Bishop being the President of the Council of Elders, called in the Greek Presbyters, and the Presbyters in the Council being at length called Prebendaries, from the allowances made to them out of the revenues of the Church for their attendance. But the name of churches was of a larger extent, being given also to single assemblies in private houses, and other places not attended with a Board of Elders, and collectively to the churches of a kingdom or nation, or in the whole world.

Thesis 7

It is therefore the duty of bishops and presbyters to govern the people according to the laws of God and the laws of the king, and in their councils to punish offenders according to those laws, and to teach those who do not know the laws of God ; but not to make new laws in the name of either God or the king.

Thesis 8

The Church is constituted, and her extent and bounds of communion are defined by the laws of God, and these laws are unchangeable.

Thesis 9

The laws of the king extend only to things that are left indifferent and undetermined by the laws of God, and particularly to the revenues and tranquillity of the Church, to her courts of justice, and to decency and order in her worship ; and all laws about things left indifferent by the laws of God ought to be referred to the civil government.

Thesis 10

The king is supreme head and governor of the Church in all things indifferent, and can nominate new bishops and presbyters to succeed in vacant places, and deprive and depose them whenever they may deserve it.

Thesis 11

The being of the Church doth not depend upon an uninterrupted succession of bishops and presbyters for governing her ; for this succession was interrupted in the time of the Babylonian captivity, until Ezra, by the commission of Artaxerxes, appointed new governors. And therefore if it should be again interrupted, the Christian people, by the authority or leave of the king, may restore it. The Christian church was also in being before there was a Christian synagogue.

Thesis 12

All persons baptized are members of Christ's body called the Church, even those who are not yet admitted into the communion of the synagogue of any city. For all members circumcised were members of the Church of the Jews in the time of the Babylonian captivity before Ezra restored their polity. And in the days of Ahab, when there remained only 7,000 in Israel who had not bowed the knee to Baal, these were the true Church of God, though without an external form of government ; and the worshippers of Baal under their external form of government were a church of idolators, such a church, as in scripture, is called the synagogue of Satan, who say they are Jews and are not, a false church with regard to the God whom they worshipped. And the 3,000 baptized by Peter were a Christian church, though they had not yet a bishop, or presbyter, or synagogue, or form of government.

Thesis 13

By imposition of hands men are admitted into the communion of the synagogue of a city, and by excommunication they are deprived of that communion, and return into the

D

state they were in by baptism alone, before they were received into communion by imposition of hands, except the sin for which they were excommunicated ; and by new imposition of hands they may be received into communion again without new baptism, and therefore by excommunication they do not lose the privilege or benefit of baptism.

Thesis 14

Men are not to be excommunicated without breaking one or more of the articles upon which they are admitted into communion. For this would be to alter the bounds of communion settled by the laws of God in the beginning of the Gospel.

Thesis 15

To impose any article of communion not imposed from the beginning is a crime of the same nature with that of those Christians of the circumcision who endeavoured to impose circumcision, and the observation of the law upon the converted Gentiles. For the law was good if a man could keep it, but we were to be saved not by the works of the law, but by faith in Jesus Christ ; and to impose those works as articles of communion, was to make them necessary to salvation, and thereby to make void the faith in Jesus Christ. And there is the same reason against imposing any other article of communion which was not imposed from the beginning. All such impositions are teaching another gospel.

Thesis 16

To refuse communion with any church or synagogue merely upon account of the laws of the king in matters indifferent, unless these laws are imposed not merely as laws of the civil government, but as articles of religion and communion, is disobedience to the king, and schism in relation to the Church.

Thesis 17

To distinguish churches from one another by any difference in customs or ceremonies, or in other laws than the Laws of God, is improper, and tends to superstitions. And if the distinction occasions a breach of communion, the person insisting upon it as a matter of religion is guilty of the schism. For the distinction being taken from things which are only of human authority and external to religion, ought not to be considered as a part of religion, nor to enter into the definition of a Church.

Thesis 18

The fundamentals or first principles of religion are the articles of communion taught from the beginning of the Gospel in catechising men in order to baptism and admission into communion ; namely, that the catechumen is to repent and forsake covetousness, ambition, and all inordinate desires of the things of this world, the flesh, and false gods called the devil, and to be baptised in the name of one God, the Father, Almighty, Maker of Heaven and Earth, and of one Lord Jesus Christ, the Son of God, and of the Holy Ghost. See Heb. v, 12, 13, 14, and vi, 1, 2, 3.

Thesis 19

After baptism we are to live according to the laws of God and the king, and to grow in grace and in the knowledge of our Lord Jesus Christ, by practising what they promised before baptism, and studying the Scriptures, and teaching one another in meekness and charity, without imposing their private opinions, or falling out about them.

Thesis 20

The commission to teach and baptize was given to the Apostles as the disciples of Christ, and to their disciples, and the disciples of their disciples, to the end of the world, there being no bishops or presbyters or church government yet instituted among the Christians. But after the institution of governments, the governors appointed men to catechise and baptize, except in cases of necessity, where the original returned. For Tertullian has told us that in his days the rule was, " In casu necessitatis quilibet laicus tingit."

QUERIES REGARDING THE WORD "HOMOOUSIOS"

Queries regarding the Word Homoousios

QUERY 1. Whether Christ sent his apostles to preach metaphysics to the unlearned common people, and to their wives and children?

QUERY 2. Whether the word ὁμοούσιος ever was in any creed before the Nicene; or any creed was produced by any one bishop at the Council of Nice for authorizing the use of that word?

QUERY 3. Whether the introducing the use of that word is not contrary to the Apostles' rule of holding fast the form of sound words?

QUERY 4. Whether the use of that word was not pressed upon the Council of Nice against the inclination of the major part of the Council?

QUERY 5. Whether it was not pressed upon them by the Emperor Constantine the Great, a catechumen not yet baptized, and no member of the Council?

QUERY 6. Whether it was not agreed by the Council that that word should, when applied to the Word of God, signify nothing more than that Christ was the express image of the Father? and whether many of the bishops, in pursuance of that interpretation of the word allowed by the Council, did not, in their subscriptions, by way of caution, add τουτ ἐστιν ὁμοούσιος?

QUERY 7. Whether Hosius (or whoever translated that Creed into Latin) did not impose upon the Western Churches by translating ὁμοούσιος by the words *unius substantiae*, instead of *consubstantialis?* and whether by that translation the Latin Churches were not drawn into an opinion that the Father and Son had one common substance, called by the Greeks *Hypostasis*,

44

and whether they did not thereby give occasion to the Eastern Churches to cry out, presently after the Council of Sardica, that the Western Churches were become Sabellian?

QUERY 8. Whether the Greeks, in opposition to this notion and language, did not use the language of three Hypostases, and whether in those days the word Hypostasis did not signify a substance?

QUERY 9. Whether the Latins did not at that time accuse all those of Arianism who used the language of three Hypostases, and thereby charge Arianism upon the Council of Nice, without knowing the true meaning of the Nicene Creed?

QUERY 10. Whether the Latins were not convinced, in the Council of Ariminum that the Council of Nice, by the word ὁμοούσιος, understood nothing more than that the Son was the express image of the Father—the acts of the Council of Nice were not produced for convincing them. And whether, upon producing the acts of that Council for proving this, the Macedonians, and some others, did not accuse the bishops of hypocrisy, who in subscribing these acts, had interpreted them by the word ὁμοούσιος in their subscriptions.

QUERY 11. Whether Athanasius, Hilary, and in general the Greeks and Latins, did not, from the time of the reign of Julian the Apostate, acknowledge the Father, Son, and Holy Ghost to be three substances, and continue to do so till the schoolmen changed the signification of the word *Hypostasis*, and brought in the notion of the three persons in one single substance?

QUERY 12. Whether the opinion of the equality of the three substances was not first set on foot in the reign of Julian the Apostate, by Athanasius, Hilary, etc.?

QUERY 13. Whether the worship of the Holy Ghost was not first set on foot presently after the Council of Sardica?

QUERY 14. Whether the Council of Sardica was not the first Council which declared for the doctrine of the Consubstantial Trinity ? and whether the Council did not affirm that there was but one hypostasis of the Father, Son, and Holy Ghost ?

QUERY 15. Whether the Bishop of Rome, five years after the death of Constantine the Great, A.C. 341, did not receive appeals from the Greek Councils, and thereby begin to usurp the universal bishopric ?

QUERY 16. Whether the Bishop of Rome, in absolving the appellants from excommunication, and communicating with them, did not excommunicate himself, and begin a quarrel with the Greek Church ?

QUERY 17. Whether the Bishop of Rome, in summoning all the bishops of the Greek Church to appear at the next Council of Rome, A.C. 342, did not challenge dominion over them, and begin to make war upon them for obtaining it ?

QUERY 18. Whether that Council of Rome, in receiving the appellants into communion, did not excommunicate themselves and support the Bishop of Rome in obtaining appeals from all the world ?

QUERY 19. Whether the Council of Sardica, in receiving the appellants into communion, and decreeing appeals from all the churches to the Bishop of Rome, did not excommunicate themselves, and become guilty of the schism which followed thereupon, and set up Papacy in all the West ?

QUERY 20. Whether the Emperor Constantine did not, by calling the Council of Milan and Aquileia, A.C. 365, abolish Popery ? and whether Hilary, Lucifer . . . were not banished for adhering to the authority of the Pope to receive appeals from the Greek Councils ?

Query 21. Whether the Emperor Gratian, A.C. 379, did not, by his edict, restore the universal bishopric of Rome over all the West ? and whether this authority of the Bishop of Rome hath not continued ever since ?

Query 22. Whether Hosius, St. Athanasius, St. Hilary, St. Ambrose, St. Hierome, St. Austin were not Papists ?

Query 23. Whether the Western Bishops, upon being convinced that the Council of Nice by the word ὁμοούσιος did [Unfinished, possibly because it would have repeated in effect Query 6. Plainly all the Queries except 1 and 2 are intended to elicit an affirmative answer].

A SHORT SCHEME OF THE TRUE RELIGION

Religion is partly fundamental and immutable, partly circumstantial and mutable. The first was the religion of Adam, Enoch, Noah, Abraham, Moses, Christ and all the saints, and consists of two parts, our duty towards God and our duty towards man, or piety and righteousness, which I will here call Godliness and Humanity.

Of Godliness

Godliness consists in the knowledge, love, and worship of God ; Humanity, in the love, righteousness, and good offices towards men. " Thou shalt love the Lord thy God with all thy heart, and with all thy soul, and with all thy mind : this is the first and great commandment, and the second is like unto it ; thou shalt love thy neighbour as thyself. On these two commandments hang all the law and the prophets." The first is enjoined in the four first commandments of the Decalogue, and the second in the six last.

Of Atheism

Opposite to the first is Atheism in profession and idolatry in practice. Atheism is so senseless and odious to mankind that it never had many professors. Can it be by accident that all birds, beasts and men have their right side and left side alike-shaped (except in their bowels), just two eyes and no more, [one] on either side the face, and just two ears, [one] on either side the head, and a nose with two holes and no more between the eyes, and one mouth under the nose, and either two fore-legs, or two wings, or two arms on the shoulders, and two legs on the hips, one on either side and no more ? Whence arises this uniformity in all their outward shapes but from the counsel and contrivance of an Author ? Whence is it that all the eyes of all sorts of living creatures are transparent to the very bottom and the only transparent members in the body, having on the outside a hard transparent skin and within transparent layers with a crystalline lens in the middle and a pupil before the lens—all of them so truly shaped and fitted for vision that no Artist can mend them? Did blind chance know that there was light and what was its refraction, and fit the eyes of all creatures after the most curious manner to make use of it?

These and such like considerations, always have, and ever will prevail with mankind, to believe that there is a Being who made all things, and has all things in his power, and who is therefore to be feared.

Idolatry

Idolatry is a more dangerous crime, because it is apt, by the authority of Kings, and under very specious pretences, to insinuate itself into mankind, kings being apt to enjoin the honour of their dead ancestors ; and it seeming very plausible to honour the souls of Heroes and Saints, and to believe that they can hear us and help us and are mediating between God and man, and reside and act principally in the temples and statues dedicated to their honour and memory. And yet, this being against the principal part of religion, is in scripture condemned and detested above all other crimes. The sin consists first in omitting the service of the true God. For the more time and devotion one spends in the worship of false gods, the less he is able to spend in that of the true one ; secondly, in serving false or feigned gods, that is, Ghosts or Spirits of dead men, or such like beings which you make your Gods, by feigning that they can hear your prayers, do you good or hurt, and praying to them for protection and blessings and trust in them for the same—and which are false gods because they have not the powers which you ascribe to them, and on which you trust. Whatever you call them—Dy, or Divi, Gods, or Saints or by any other name is not material. If you ascribe such powers to them and put such trust in them, as the heathens ascribed to and put in their gods, you make them such gods as the heathens worshipped, and as are forbidden in the first commandment.

St. Paul tells the heathens that the gods which they worshipped were not Gods. He does not mean that they were not infinite, eternal, omnipotent and omniscient (for the heathens did not take them to be such), but he means they were not such gods as the heathens believed them to be, that is, spirits able to hear and see their worshippers and do them good or hurt. To place such powers in the souls of dead men is that doctrine of devils or demons condemned by the Apostle. An idol is nothing in the world, a vanity, a lie, a fictitious power.

The Egyptians and other heathens who propagated Idolatry believed the transmigration of souls, and accordingly taught that the souls of men after death went into several subjects as the Ox, Apis, and other sacred animals of Egypt, into the sun, moon, and stars, into images consecrated to them etc., and on this opinion grounded their worship of those subjects, supposing that the stars by these intelligences were moved in their orbs, and understood and governed human affairs, and that statues by these spirits could hear and help us, and sometimes move themselves and give oracles. And these are the devils or demons which idolators worshipped (Lev. vii, 7, Deut. xxxii, 17, 2 Chron. xi, 15, Psal. cvi, 37, 1 Cor. x, 20, Rev. ix, 20) and whose worship the prophets upbraid with folly by representing that the idols can neither hear nor see nor walk, that is, that they are not animated by such souls as those by which men hear and see and walk, but are mere inanimate stocks and stones void of all life and power.

So covetous men, by putting that trust in riches which they should put in God become a sort of idolators. And much more plainly is it idolatrous to trust in charms, ceremonies, dead bodies, consecrated substances and the like. All this is worshipping the creation instead of the creator.

And, thirdly, the sin of idolatry consists in making and worshipping the images of dead men, or of other things in heaven above or in the earth beneath or in the waters below the earth— that is, of birds, beasts, or fishes (contrary to the second commandment) upon a supposition that, by virtue of the souls of dead men, or of the supreme God or any other spirits or demons good or bad inhabiting them, or upon any other account, they can hear and see their worshippers or do them good or hurt. To ascribe such powers to them is to feign them gods (such gods as the heathens worshipped) and to love or fear or trust in them, or express such love, fear, or trust by prayers, praises, thanksgiving, sacrifices, adorations, or any other outward action or service is the idolatry of the old heathens forbidden in the second commandment. Stones and stocks have no such powers ; they are not inhabited by the souls of dead men. " Eyes have they and see not, ears have they and hear not " ; they are vanities, lies, fictitious powers, and on this account they are called false gods, and derided as such by all the Prophets. And of the same kind of folly is it to place any trust in the bodies or bones of dead men, or in things consecrated, or other things without life, or in any ceremonies or charms—for even the trusting in riches is by the Apostle called idolatry.

We are therefore to acknowledge one God, infinite, eternal, omnipresent, omniscient, and omnipotent, the creator of all things, most wise, most just, most good, most holy, and to have no other gods but him. We must love him, fear him, honour him, trust in him, pray to him, give him thanks, praise him, hallow his name, obey his commandments, and set times apart for his service, as we are directed in the third and fourth commandments. " For this is the love of God, that we keep his commandments, and his commandments are not grievous." 1 John v, 3.

These things we must do, not to any mediator between him and us, but to him alone, "that he may give his angels charge over us," who, being our fellow-servants, are pleased with the worship which we give to their God. And this is the first and principal part of religion. This always was and always will be the religion of all God's people from the beginning to the end of the world.

Of Humanity

The other part of the true religion is our duty to man. We must love our neighbours as ourselves, we must be charitable to all men, for charity is the greatest of graces, greater then even faith or hope and covers a multitude of sins. We must be righteous, and do to all men as we would that they should do to us. In politics *Salus populi suprema lex ;* in private concerns *Quod tibi fieri non vis alteri nec fieri* were acknowledged by heathens and are or ought to be the laws of all mankind. This was the Ethics, or good manners, taught the first ages by Noah and his sons by their seven precepts, the heathens by Socrates, Confucius and other philosophers, the Israelites by Moses and the Prophets and the Christians more fully by Christ and his Apostles. This is that law which the Apostle tells you was written in the hearts of the Gentiles, and by which they were to be judged in the last day. Romans ii, 12, 14, 15, also Romans i, ii. Thus you see there is but one law for all nations, the law of righteousness and charity dictated to the Christians by Christ, to the Jews by Moses, and to all mankind by the light of reason, and by this law all men are to be judged at the last day. Romans ii. This was the religion of the first ages till they forsook the right worship of the true God and turned aside to the worship of dead men and idols, and their God gave them over to their lusts and passions for working all manner of unrighteousness. But Moses made a reformation among the Israelites, not from the ancient religion propagated by Noah and his posterity to the nations but from the idolatry and immorality with which the nations had corrupted themselves. For as many of the heathens as were converted from their corruptions to only the true God, and followed the law of righteousness were admitted by the Jews into their Gates and outward court of the Temple as Proselytes, though they did not receive the law of Moses. The Jews rejected not the Religion of Noah and the first nations, but proselyted the heathens to it as to the true ancient religion, though a religion, which they accounted not so perfect as that of

Moses. And in like manner we may lawfully proselyte heathens to it, that is, to purity and righteousness, and ought to value and love those who profess and practise it, even though they do not yet believe in Christ, for it is the true religion of Christians as well as heathens, though not all the true Christian religion. 'Tis so great and necessary a part of the Christian religion that the righteousness of the saints is the white clothing of the Lamb's wife, Apoc. xix, 8, and the righteous go into eternal life, Matt. xxv, 46, and as Christ is righteous so every one that hath righteousness is born of God, 1 John ii, 29. Abel was righteous, Hebs. xi, 4 ; Matt. xxiii, 35 ; 1 John iii, 12, and Noah was a preacher of righteousness, 2 Peter ii, 5, and by his righteousness was saved from the flood, Gen. vii, 1. Christ is called the righteous, 1 John ii, 1, and by his righteousness we are saved, Rom. iii, 25 ; v, 18 ; 1 Cor. i, 30 ; and except our righteousness exceed the righteousness of the Scribes and Pharisees we shall not enter into the kingdom of heaven, Matt. v. 20. Righteousness is the religion of the kingdom of heaven, 2 Peter iii, 13 ; Isaiah lx, 21, and even the property of God himself (Jud. vi, ii ; 1 Sam. xii, 7 ; Ezra ix, 15 ; Nehem. ix, 8 ; Ps. cxix, 137) towards man. Righteousness and love are inseparable, for he that loveth another hath fulfilled the law, Romans xiii, 8-10. He that loveth his brother abideth in the light and there is no occasion of stumbling in him. 1 John ii, 10 ; See 1 John iii, 14, 15 ; 1 John iv, 1 Cor. xiii.

[RELIGION. THREE PARAGRAPHS]

Our Religion to God

God made the world and governs it invisibly, and hath commanded us to love, honour and worship him and no other God but him, and to do it without making any image of him, and not to name him idly and without reverence, and to honour our parents, masters and governors, and love our neighbours as ourselves, and to be temperate, modest, just and peaceable, and to be merciful even to brute beasts.

Our Religion to Jesus Christ

Jesus Christ, a true man born of a woman, was crucified by the Jews for teaching them the truth, and, by the same power by which God gave life at the first to every species of animals, being revived, he appeared to his disciples and explained to them Moses and the Prophets concerning himself, as that he was the Son of righteousness spoken of by Malachi, the son of man and the Messiah spoken of by Daniel,[1] the servant of God and lamb of God and Redeemer spoken of by Isaiah, the Son of God and the Holy one spoken of by David, the seed of the woman and the Prophet and the Shiloh spoken of by Moses etc. And then he sent his disciples to teach others what he had taught them, and is gone into the heavens to receive a kingdom and prepare a place for us, and is mystically said to sit at the right hand of God, that is, to be next to him in dignity, and is worshipped and glorified as the Lamb of God, and hath sent the Holy Ghost to comfort us in his absence, and will at length return and reign above (invisible to mortals) till he hath raised up and judged all the dead, the saints in the first thousand

[1] He is God's servant David spoken of by Ezekiel, the Lord our righteousness spoken of by Jeremiah, the Ruler in Israel spoken of by Micah.

years and the rest afterwards, and sent the wicked to places suitable to their merits. And then he will give up this kingdom to the Father, and carry the blessed (whom he hath merited by his death and redeemed with his blood) to the place, or mansion, which he is now preparing for them, for in God's house (which is the universe) are many mansions.

Our Religion to the Church

We enter into Societies (called churches), not by birth as the Jews did, but by the ceremonies of baptism, confirmation, and assemble weekly to worship God jointly by prayers and praises, and in our assemblies commemorate the death of Christ by breaking of bread and drinking of wine—the symbols of his body and blood—and submit our causes to our governors, who in every city compose a board of Elders with a President elected by the citizens under whom our Deacons take care of the poor. And every particular church sends an Elder or Presbyter to every Parish under its jurisdiction to instruct and govern the inhabitants. And by communicatory letters from the President they join in worship with other cities, all which together compose the Church catholic. And this Church was illuminated by the lamps of the seven Churches of Asia till the death of John the Apostle and his disciples, and had authority to propagate what she received, and only what she received by tradition from the Apostles and Prophets, and is to continue till the times of the Gentiles be accomplished, and then shall all Israel be saved.

[TWELVE ARTICLES]

ART. 1. There is one God, the Father, ever living, omnipresent, omniscient, almighty, the maker of heaven and earth, and one mediator between God and man, the man Christ Jesus.[1]

ART. 2. The Father is the invisible God whom no eye hath seen, or can see. All other beings are sometimes visible.

ART. 3. The Father hath life in himself, and hath given the Son to have life in himself.

ART. 4. The Father is omniscient, and hath all knowledge originally in his own breast, and communicates knowledge of future things to Jesus Christ ; and none in heaven or earth, or under the earth, is worthy to receive knowledge of future things immediately from the Father but the Lamb. And therefore, the testimony of Jesus is the spirit of prophecy, and Jesus is the Word or prophet of God.

ART. 5. The Father is immovable, no place being capable of becoming emptier or fuller of him than it is by the eternal necessity of nature. All other beings are movable from place to place.

ART. 6. All the worship (whether of prayer, praise, or thanksgiving) which was due to the Father before the coming of Christ is still due to him. Christ came not to diminish the worship of his Father.

ART. 7. Prayers are most prevalent when directed to the Father in the name of the Son.

[1 This Article is based on 1 Timothy ii, 5, " For there is one God, and one Mediator between God and man, the man Christ Jesus," a text which may still be read inscribed on the wall of a Unitarian Chapel].

ART. 8. We are to return thanks to the Father alone for creating us, and giving us food and raiment and other blessings of this life, and whatsoever we are to thank him for, or desire that he would do for us, we ask of him immediately in the name of Christ.

ART. 9. We need not pray to Christ to intercede for us. If we pray the Father aright, he will intercede.

ART. 10. It is not necessary to salvation to direct our prayers to any other than the Father in the name of the Son.

ART. 11. To give the name of God to angels or kings is not against the First Commandment. To give the worship of the God of the Jews to angels or kings, is against it. The meaning of the commandment is, Thou shalt worship no other God but me.

ART. 12. " To us there is but one God, the Father, of whom are all things, and one Lord Jesus Christ, by whom are all things, and we by him "—That is, we are to worship the Father alone as God Almighty, and Jesus alone as the Lord, the Messiah, the Great King, the Lamb of God who was slain, and hath redeemed us with his blood, and made us kings and priests.

[" All things " in 1 Cor. viii, 6 (cited in the last Article) is interpreted by Socinians as " things which pertain to Christians " (Racovian Catechism Trans. by T. Rees, p. 133) not as by Arians of all creation. Commenting on Colossians i, 15 the Catechism similarly interprets Christ " the first born of every creature " as " the first of the new creation" i.e., Christians, adding, " That the Lord Jesus was the first of the things made in the old creation our opponents cannot admit unless they would become Arians."]

E

[SEVEN STATEMENTS ON RELIGION]

1. That religion and Philosophy are to be preserved distinct. We are not to introduce divine revelations into Philosophy nor philosophical opinions into religion.

2. Men are not to be deprived of communion without violating the conditions upon which they were admitted into communion.

3. That Religion and polity, or the laws of God and the laws of man, are to be kept distinct. We are not to make the commandments of men a part of the laws of God.

4. The conditions or articles of communion are those which in the primitive Church were taught the Catechumens in order to baptism and imposition of hand, viz. to forsake the Devil and all his works, to abstain from the lusts of the flesh, the lusts of the eye, and pride ; repentance, and abstinence from dead works, and a practical belief in one God, the Father, one Lord, Jesus Christ, and in the Holy Ghost.

5. By dead works we are to understand idolatry, lusts of the flesh, covetousness and ambition. We are to forsake the Devil and his works, that is, false gods and idols with the works which accompany such worship, as being contrary to the love of God, and we are to refrain from the lust of the flesh, the lust of the eye, and the pride of life, that is, from inordinate desires of the flesh and from covetousness and ambition—as being contrary to the love of our neighbour. And we are to believe aright in one God and one Christ, and in the Holy Ghost, and be baptized in their name, and to love our neighbour as ourselves ; and being admitted into the communion of some particular Church by the governors thereof, upon these conditions, we are not to be deprived of that communion without breach of these conditions.

58

6. By communion, I understand a fellowship in the worship of that Church, so as to join with them in their public prayers, praises, thanksgivings, and in celebrating the Eucharist ; and by excommunication, a deprivation of that communion.

7. This communion men are to be admitted into and deprived of by order of the board of the governors of that Church, and the Order is properly to be declared by the President of the Board and the Declaration may be accompanied with some ceremony, as of imposition of hands by the president in cases of admission or re-admission, or of swinging down a torch in cases of excommunication. The Declaration by imposition of hands is a Jewish ceremony. We call it confirmation, meaning a confirmation of what was done by the God-fathers in bringing the Infant.

8. [Unfinished].

PARADOXICAL QUESTIONS CONCERNING THE MORALS AND ACTIONS OF ATHANASIUS AND HIS FOLLOWERS

PREFACE

The Catalogue of Newton Papers reports (p.73) that of the " Paradoxical Questions " there are " Drafts of various Portions, some in several states, in all about 30,000 words on 120 pp., unnumbered and confused . . . and many sheets imperfect." Brewster (*Memoirs* II, 272) quotes from a copy which he describes in a footnote as " written in Sir Isaac's own hand and extends to sixty-two folio pages. It wants the last leaf." He adds that in the Catalogue of Newton MSS. made in 1777 by Bishop Horsley and his colleague two copies of this MS. are mentioned in one place and elsewhere another mentioned as complete, " shewing that the other two were not so." The MS. belonging to the King's College Collection is undoubtedly complete, and written by Newton, except a sentence added at the end in pencil by another hand.

The evidence relating to MSS. is important as proving the time and labour given by the writer to this subject. The MS. here copied is beautifully written and amply documented. It was named by Mrs. Conduitt amongst those she desired to be published.

Here is a sustained, closely reasoned attempt to prove, in the words of Lord Keynes, " the dishonesty and falsification of records for which St. Athanasius was responsible," and it is marked by a vein of irony. The result is a portrait of the fourth century theologian and interpretations of events in which he was the principal actor in strong contrast with those given by historians from the 18th century to our own day. It is " Newton " (not Athanasius) " contra mundum," though in 1749 Whiston (*Memoirs* p.601) described Athanasius as " a notorious Forger and Lyar."

PARADOXICAL QUESTIONS

Concerning the Morals and Actions of Athanasius and his Followers

Quest. I.

Whether the ignominious death of Arius in a boghouse was not a story feigned and put about by Athanasius above twenty years after his death ?

How Arius died I reckon a question of no moment, but because it leads to other things of moment, I choose to begin with it.

We are told in history that he was excommunicated by the council of Nice, banished by the Emperor Constantine the Great, and some time after released out of banishment by the same Emperor, and that he died at Constantinople in a boghouse miserably by the effusion of his bowels the day before he was to have been absolved from excommunication. Now this story of his death was not spread abroad till about 24 years after his death, and then it was first vented by his greatest enemy, Athanasius, in a clandestine way. For Athanasius in the end of the reign of Constantius, being forced to retire from his bishopric into the wilderness of Egypt, broached that story there by sending about a narrative of it in a timorous and cautious manner, charging them not to transcribe it but to return it back to him so soon as they had read it. And this appears by a letter which he sent about the same time to those Monks in which he writes thus : " For the full condemnation and rejection of the heresy of the Arians ye are to believe that the judgment of God in the death of Arius is sufficient, which ye have even now learnt from others. For what God has constituted let no man annul ; and whom he has condemned, who shall pronounce just ? For who from so great a sign knows not that the heresy is hated of God notwithstanding that it is defended of men ? When therefore you have read it, pray for

us, and exhort one another to it, and straitway send back these
things to us and publish no copy thereof, nor transcribe any for
yourselves, but be ye content as just usurers with the bare
reading of it, although ye may desire to read it often.   For it is
not safe that those our writings should come to posterity which
we composed as babblers and unlearned." Thus far Athanasius.
In this epistle he mentions his own flight and the placing of
George in the chair of Alexandria, which happened A.C. 356.
He mentions also the subscription of Liberius, A.C. 358, and
both the lapse and death of Hosius, the first of which happened
at Sirmium A.C. 357, and the last in or after the Council of
Ariminum, as Baronius proves ; and therefore this epistle was
written between the Council of Ariminum and death of Constantius, and by consequence A.C. 359 or soon after, that is,
24 years after the ignominious death of Arius, or above.   For he
died, according to the relation of Athanasius, before the Council
of Tyre which met A.C. 335, or, according to the relation of the
ecclesiastical historians, soon after the Council of Ariminum sat
A.C. 339.

Now at the same time this libel or narrative of the death of
Arius went about in the wilderness among the Monks, one
Serapion, upon a dispute whether Arius died in communion
with the Church, wrote to Athanasius to know his opinion about
it ; to whom Athanasius returned this answer :[1]
" I have read the letters of your Reverence in which you
desire that I would write to you those things which are at
this time done against me, and concerning the wicked heresy
of Arius, by which we suffer these things, and how Arius ended
his life.   Two of these three requests I have willingly performed
and sent to your piety what I have written to the Monks, for
thence you may learn what relates both to the troubles and to
the heresy.   But concerning the third head, namely, the death
of Arius, I much doubted with myself about it fearing lest in
doing it, I should seem to exult over the death of the man.   But
yet because a disputation amongst you concerning the heresy

[1] " Festal Epistola in operibus Athanasii et apud Theodoritum Eccl. l. i, c. 14."

ended in this question " Whether Arius died in communion with the Church ?", for ending the dispute about his death I will tell you the truth, accounting it the same thing to tell this as to end the contention, for I persuade myself that the miracle of his death being known, it will no longer be doubted whether the Arian heresy be odious to God or not. Truly I was not at Constantinople when he died, but Macarius the Presbyter was there, and I learnt it by his relation. Arius, by the endeavour of the Eusebians, being called to the Emperor Constantine, and at his entrance being asked by the Emperor, if he kept the faith of the Catholic Church, affirmed upon oath that he believed aright, suppressing what he had been excommunicated for by Alexander his bishop and colouring over his profession with scripture expressions. When therefore he had sworn that he had done none of those things for which he was by Alexander excommunicated, the Emperor dismissed him with these words : " If thy faith be right, thou hast well sworn, but if impious and yet thou hast sworn, God will condemn thee for thy oath." Him therefore thus departing from the Emperor the Eusebians, by their usual force, would have introduced into the Church, but Alexander bishop of Constantinople contradicted it saying that the inventor of a heresy ought not to be received into communion. Then the Eusebians threatened saying : " As we have procured against your will that he should be called by the Emperor, so tomorrow, notwithstanding 'tis against your mind, we will bring Arius into communion with us in this Church. It was the Sabbath (that is, Saturday) when they said this, which Alexander hearing and being much troubled he went into the Church, and lifting up his hands to God, lamented, and falling upon his face on the ground, prayed. Macarius was then present praying with him and hearing his words. Now he requested one of these things. " If Arius," saith he, " must to-morrow be brought into the congregation, let thy servant now depart and destroy not the righteous with the wicked ; but if thou wilt spare thy Church (for I know thou wilt spare it) look upon the words of the Eusebians and give not thy inheritance into destruction and disgrace, and take away Arius lest, he being received into the Church, his heresy may seem also to be received with him, and so impiety be counted for piety." The Bishop, having thus prayed, went thence very thoughtful, and there followed a thing wonderful and incredible. For the Eusebians threatening, the Bishop prayed, but Arius, confiding in the Eusebians and prating much, went into a bog-house as if to ease himself, and suddenly (as 'tis written) falling headlong burst in sunder, and died upon the ground, being deprived both of communion and life. Such was the end of Arius. And the Eusebians, being greatly ashamed, buried their fellow-conspirator, but the Church rejoicing, Alexander celebrated the communion in piety and sound faith with all the brethren praying and greatly glorifying God : not as if he rejoiced at his death (far be it, for it is appointed all men once to die) but because this thing appeared above all human judgment, for the Lord himself judging between the threatenings of the Eusebians and the prayer of Alexander, condemned the Arian heresy, shewing it unworthy of the communion of the Church, and manifesting to all men that although it be countenanced by the Emperor and by all mortals yet 'tis condemned by the Church. Certainly many of those who were deceived before were converted namely because God himself had condemned the heresy and shown it to be incommunicable to the Church. Wherefore let the Question cease among you. To them who moved this question let this be read, together with what I wrote in brief to the Monks concerning this heresy, that they, being thence instructed, may more and more condemn it. But let no copy of these things be transcribed, nor transcribe any for yourself. For this I have also enjoined the Monks. But according to your candour, if anything be wanting in the writings, add it, and straitway return them to us."—Thus far Athanasius.

So then the story of Arius's death was first broached by Athanasius at that time when Arianism was countenanced by the Emperor and by all mortals, and, by consequence, after the compliance of the western Bishops in the Council of Ariminum : and Athanasius pretended no other author for it than Macarius—a dead man, and propounded it amongst his ignorant and credulous Monks with much timorousness, charging them to return the writings quickly to him without letting any copies be taken lest it should at length get into such hands as he could not trust, for saith he, " it is not safe that it should come to posterity." But a while after, when the story was once spread abroad so that he might tell it without danger of being reputed its author, he tells it again in his first Oration without any such caution.

Now the reasons which make me suspect the truth of this story are these :

1. Because the prayer of Macarius is contrary to the temper and spirit of true Christianity, and it is not likely that God would hear a wicked prayer.

2. Because the story came to us not from Constantinople as it ought to have done, but from Egypt, and was not broached there till 24 years after the death of Arius, or above. Athanasius and the Bishops of Egypt, when collected in a Council at Alexandria five years after the Council of Tyre, knew nothing of it, as you may perceive by the letter which that Council wrote in defence of Athanasius against Arius and the Council of Tyre. Nor did Julius, Bishop of Rome, know anything of it when he wrote in defence of Athanasius. Nor did the Council of Sardica (where Athanasius and his friends were assembled together out of all the Empire) know anything of it, as you may perceive by their letters. Athanasius long after these times told it as a secret, and out of his writings the ecclesiastical historians have propagated it to posterity.

3. Because it was broached and spread abroad by the grand enemy of Arius without any pretence of proof or other evidence than the credit of the reporter, for detracting stories never look well when told by professed enemies. Such a person may be an accuser but not a witness, and accusations without proof are

by the general rule of all courts of justice to be accounted calumnies.

4. Because Athanasius broached it, as he confesseth, to blast the name and religion of his enemies, and that at a time when he was reduced to the greatest despair.

5. Because he broached it in a clandestine way in the wilderness amongst the Monks of his own party who were ignorant of the affairs of the world and depended on his mouth as on an oracle : and also because he was fearful lest the writings by which he broached it should come into other hands which he could not trust, or remain upon record. "For," saith he, " 'tis not safe that they should come to posterity."

6. Because the story, after he had broached it, spread but slowly, being not generally known till the ecclesiastical historians about ninety years after the death of Arius set it down in their histories as Theodoret (Eccles. Hist. L.i. c.13) informs us. Sulpicius Severus, who wrote his history above thirty years after, knew nothing of it. It seems to have made little noise in the world before the Greek historians met with it in the writings of Athanasius, and put it about.

7. And though it came originally from Egypt and was not known in the world till about 24 years after the death of Arius, yet Athanasius, to give credit to it amongst the ·Egyptian monks, told it then and there as if it had been well known at Constantinople from the beginning, saying that at the ignominious death of Arius the Eusebians were ashamed and many of them were converted and the Church rejoiced greatly. For how it could be publicly known there at the first, and not spread thence into Egypt and other regions before Athanasius told it I understand not.

Lastly, the main design of the story is to represent that Arius died miserably without the pale of the Church, and for that end Athanasius, in his letter to Serapion, represents as if he died at Constantinople immediately after he was recalled thither from banishment before the Eusebians had time enough to receive him into communion. And in his letter to the Monks when he had mentioned the ignominious death of Arius he subjoins that the Eusebians not very long after accomplished what they had been endeavouring at Constantinople, receiving the Arians into communion (meaning at Jerusalem) and pretending the Emperor's command, and not blushing, after the deposition of Athanasius, to write in their letters (that is, in a letter of the Council of Jerusalem to Alexandria) that envy was ceased and that they had received the Arians and boasted the Emperor's command for it, not fearing to add that the faith of the Arians was right.

Thus does Athanasius in these his two letters, that he may make Arius die without the pale of the Church, place his death at Constantinople before the Arians were received at Jerusalem. And yet it is certain that Arius went from Constantinople to Tyre and Jerusalem and Alexandria before he died, and was one of those whom the Council of Jerusalem received into communion, for Constantine the Great recalled him and Euzoius from banishment, and, after he had allowed their profession of faith, sent them to the Council of Tyre to be received into communion, and that Council, (which Eusebius represents a greater Council than that at Nice) removing to Jerusalem, received them there, and sent them with a reccomendatory letter to Alexandria to be re-admitted to their places. This story is told not only by the Ecclesiastical Historians,[1] but also by the Bishops of that Council itself in that letter, and by the Bishops of that Council met again in the Council of Antioch, where they write that they, being judges of the faith of Arius, had received him rather than followed him. 'Tis acknowledged also by Athanasius himself in his book "De Synodis Ariminii et Seleuciae" where he recites the letter of the Council of Jerusalem, and then adds that that Council, "after the banishment of Athanasius, wrote in this letter to Alexandria that they should receive Arius and those that were with him." And the

[1] Socrates L.i, C.26, 27, 33, 37, 38 : Sozom L.ii, C.27-29 : Ruffin L.i, C.11.

memory and tradition of his reception at Tyre remained in Egypt till Athanasius, by a contrary story, extinguished it, as is manifest by the opposition that the story of the death of Arius met with at first ; some disputing that he died in communion till Athanasius commanded them silence. Historians, therefore, finding that Arius was certainly received at Tyre and went thence to Alexandria, endeavoured to mend the narrative of Athanasius by placing the death of Arius not immediately after his return from banishment to Constantinople, as Athanasius doth, but after his return from Alexandria thither. And yet to allow, as they do, that Arius was received into communion at Jerusalem and, by consequence, died within the pale of the Church, is contrary to the design of the story. And to tell that the Eusebians, after they had received him at Jerusalem, would have received him at Constantinople as if they had not received him before is contrary not only to the narrative of Athanasius but also to common sense. From one excommunication there is but one absolution.

These are the reasons which incline me to suspect the story of the death of Arius, and whilst (? since) Athanasius wrote his book " De Synodis Ariminii et Seleuciae " long after the death of Macarius, and therein relates the reception of Arius at Jerusalem : I suspect also that he knew nothing then of the story of Arius dying out of communion, and therefore had it not from Macarius as he pretends, but invented it himself.

Quest. II.

Whether the Meletians deserved that ill character which Athanasius gave them.

In Diocletian's persecution there arose a controversy between Peter the Bishop of Alexandria and Meletius the first of the Bishops under him ; which caused a schism in the churches of Egypt ; both parties notwithstanding keeping communion with the Churches abroad. When Athanasius succeeded in the Bishopric of Alexandria, he was accused of tyrannical behaviour towards the Meletians, so as in the time of the sacrament to break the communion cup of one Ischyras, a Meletian Presbyter in Mareotis. Whereupon the Meletians accusing Athanasius of these things, he was tried and condemned in the Council of Tyre, and banished by the Emperor Constantine the Great. And this caused great enmity between Athanasius and the Meletians. Athanasius therefore in his Second Apology gives this character of Meletius, that he was by Peter the Bishop of Alexandria, in a common synod of the Bishops, convicted of many crimes, and particularly that he had sacrificed to idols and for these things deposed, and that he thereupon made a schism, so that his followers instead of Christians were called Meletians. But Epiphanius (Haer. 68) relates the origin of the schism much otherwise. For he calls Meletius a Confessor, and saith that when he and Peter and other martyrs and Confessors were in prison together, there arose a dispute about the reception of lapsed persons, Peter, out of mercy, being for a speedy reception and Meletius and Pelrus and many other martyrs and confessors, out of zeal for piety, being for a competent time of penitence before being received, so that the sincerity of their penitence might first appear : and thereupon they divided ; the greater part following Meletius. Afterwards Peter suffered martyrdom, and Meletius for some time was condemned to the mines. Thus Epiphanius.

Now that which makes me suspect the relation of Athanasius is first because the character given by the greatest enemy is always the most to be suspected, and then because the Council of Nice did not receive Meletius and his party into communion as they would have done had they been excommunicate before, but without any absolution continued them in their bishoprics, and only for putting an end to the schism confined Meletius to his city and deprived him of the power of ordaining, as you may see in the epistle of this Council to the Churches of Egypt (Apud Theodoritum L.i, c.6). For if Meletius and his party continued in communion without even being absolved from excommunications (as it is plain by the epistle of the Council of Nice that they did) then they were never excommunicate ; and if so, then the story of Athanasius about their being excommunicate for various crimes is a fiction.

Quest. III.

Whether the Council of Tyre and Jerusalem was not an orthodox authentic Council bigger than that of Nice.

The friends of Athanasius endeavour all they can to diminish the credit of this Council, and make it a conventicle of a few Bishops selected by his enemies for oppressing him. So Socrates tells us it consisted of but sixty Bishops. And yet, by considering earlier records, I suspect it was as big or bigger than the Council of Nice. For the design of this Council being very great, it needed great credit and authority to support it. They were not only to examine the cause [case] of Athanasius, but also to receive into communion Arius and Euzoius with their followers in Egypt, as men who had been oppressed by a false representation of their faith : and it was an ancient[1] Canon of the Church as well as a necessary one that no man should be received by a less number of Bishops than those by which he had been ejected. And therefore the Emperor sent his letters into all the Eastern Empire requiring the attendance of the Bishops that the Council might be full. For this, the eighty Eastern Bishops in the letter which at their return from the Council of Sardica they wrote at Philippopolis, affirm in these words. " Concilium . . . post alterum annum in Tyro propter Athanasii facinora necessario iterum celebratur. Advenerunt Episcopi de Macedonia et de Pannonia, Bithynia et omnibus partibus Orientis, Imperatoris jussione constricti." The Eastern Bishops objected against Athanasius that, by returning to his bishopric without being restored by as many Bishops as had deposed him, he had violated the ancient Canon : but the friends of Athanasius never retorted the accusation upon the Eastern

---

[1] " Concilium Antiochenum in Epist. ad Julium Papam."

Bishops as if they had broken the same Canon in receiving the Arians at Tyre. In the times next after the Council the Athanasians never excepted against it for not being big enough. They never desired that a fuller Council should be called in the East to examine the Acts of this : but, as if a fuller could not well be called there, or, if called, would not be for their advantage, they appealed to the West. And thereupon arose a quarrel, not between the West and a few Bishops of the East, but between the Eastern and Western churches, as is plain by the schism which was thereby made soon after between them. But let us hear how Eusebius, who was in both Councils and so is a good witness, describes this and compares it with the other. For he tells us[1] how the remoter regions of Macedonia, Pannonia, Moesia, and Persia sent their Metropolitans thither, and then adds "Bithynia quoque et Thraces prœsentia sua conventum ornabant, nec deerant e Ciliciæ Episcopis clarissimi quiqe. Ex Cappodocia item qui doctrina et elo- quentia praestabant in medio consessu enituerunt. Adhuc Syria omnis, Mesopotamia, Phenice, Arabia et Palestina ; ipsa Egyptus quoque ac Libya ac qui Thebaidem incolunt, omnes in unum congregati magnum illum Dei Chorum imple- bant. Quos ex omnibus Provinciis innumerabilis hominum multitudo sequebatur." And a little after : " Hance secundam synodum omnium quas novimus maximam, Imperator Hierosolymis congregavit, post primam illam quam in urbe Bithyniae nobilissima collegerat. Sed illa quidem triumphalis erat ; in imperii vicennalibus preces ac vota pro victoria de hostibus parta in urbe victoriae cognomino persolvens. Haec vero tricennalium festivitatem ornavit cum Imperator Deo omnium bonorum authori, Martyrium velut quoddam pacis donarium in ipso servatoris nostri monumento dedicaret." Thus far Eusebius, giving the pre-eminence to the latter Synod as being called upon the more holy and solemn occasion to celebrate the Emperor's greatest year.

This Council has been reputed Arian, and on that account

[1] " Euseb. in vita Constant. L.4, c.43, 47, ex versione Valesii."

of no authority, but the accusation was never proved, and
an accusation without proof is of no credit.   The accusation,
indeed, has gained credit among the followers of Athanasius
for a long time : but this makes it no more than popular fame,
and popular fame without original evidence, though of two
thousand years standing is but popular fame, nor can any man
readily take up with it without making himself one of the giddy
mobile. Such fame, indeed, when the original of it is forgotten,
may make a strong presumption, but when we know the original,
and see that it was spread abroad without evidence can be of
no moment. Wise men must look only to the evidence. Now
all the evidence that this Council was Arian is only this—that
they received Arius into communion and banished Athanasius.
This is all the ground upon which the fame of their being
Arian was spread abroad by the mobile of Athanasius his party,
and this is no just ground at all, for they did not receive Arius
without his disowning those things for which he had been
condemned at Nice, nor condemned Athanasius for his owning
the Nicene decrees : and 'tis not the receiving or condemning
men but the receiving or condemning opinions that can make
any Council heretical. So far was this Council from being
Arian that the Bishops thereof in almost all their following
Councils declared against Arianism, and anathematized the
opinions for which Arius had been condemned. If you say
they dissembled and were Arians in their heart while they were
orthodox in their language, I must ask you how you or any man
else can know that. For an accusation, without knowledge of
the thing is that which the world calls clamour calumny and
malice. Had Athanasius and his Monks the gift of searching
and knowing men's hearts ? and is this a ground for us to rely
upon ? We have no other means of knowing men's faith but
by their profession and outward communion and way of worship,
and by all these characters the fathers of this Council were
orthodox. They constantly professed against Arianism and
were in communion with the Churches of all the world, and
worshipped as other Christians of that age did. For they were

never reprehended by their enemies upon any of these heads.
Should any Church of our age charge heresy upon any body of
men of her own communion, and should the men reply that
they always were of the communion of that Church and always
professed her faith and used her worship, and that they still
continue in that profession and practice, and should the accusers
grant all this and only reply that notwithstanding their
communion, profession and practice they were heretics in their
hearts ; and should the Judges upon this accusation condemn
them to death : I think such proceedings would by all sober
men be accounted as malicious and barbarous as any we ever
heard of. And yet this seems to be case of the Council of Tyre,
who without any proof are accused of heresy by those of their
own communion contrary to their constant profession and
practice and their authority murdered upon the accusation.

If you say that the fathers of the Council of Tyre did afterwards in the Councils of Ariminum and Seleucia declare for
Arianism, I answer that you may with better reason say that they
declared against Arianism in the Council of Nice, or, if you
please, that the Nicene Council was Arian because the Tyrian
was so. For the Councils of Nice and Tyre, being great and general Councils of the one and the same Greek Church collected
within the space of ten years under one and the same Emperor,
have a far greater affinity with one another than the Councils of
Tyre and Seleucia collected under different Emperors at the
distance of 23 years. If some of the Tyrian Fathers were at
Seleucia, many more of the Nicene were at Tyre. This Council,
being collected so soon after that of Nice, consisted partly of
the Nicene Fathers and partly of their immediate disciples and
successors : nor had Constantine the Great done anything to
make the Fathers of the Greek Churches alter their opinion
between these two Councils : and therefore to accuse the
Tyrian Council of Arianism is in effect to say that the generality
of the Nicene Fathers were Arians in their hearts, and dissembled
in their subscriptions. For they refused to subscribe against
Arius till Constantine came in person into the Council to

F

overcome them, and then they subscribed with reserves. But between the times of the Councils of Tyre and Seleucia there was time enough for Constantine to work a change in the Bishops and Constantius was the more likely man to work it, so that if there was any change wrought in the Greek Bishops between the Councils of Nice and Seleucia it is much more reasonable to believe that Constantius wrought it after the Council of Tyre than Constantine before.

But what if some of the Tyrian Bishops—what if many of them were Arians ? Does this invalidate the authority of the Council of Tyre ? surely not. The Athanasians sometimes complain as if the Eusebians dissembled in the Council of Nice, but yet would never allow that the authority of that Council was invalidated thereby. The authority of a Judge depends not upon his religion or sincerity but upon his incorporation into the body politic and upon his Commission to act. And so the authority of a Council depends not upon the secret religion and sincerity of the men, but upon their being in external communion with the Church Catholic, and having a legal commission to meet and act in Council. For otherwise we could never be certain that any Council is authentic. And upon this ground the Council of Tyre was as authentic as any Greek Council ever was or could be since the Apostles' days, they being in communion with the Church Catholic and legally convened by the letters of Constantine the Great.

Now that this was an authentic Council is manifest also by the consent of all parties in that age. For Athanasius and his party in that age questioned not the authority of this Council, but only complained as if they had abused their authority by corrupt judgment. They endeavoured, by fixing the imputation of Arius upon them, not to invalidate their authority but to bring their sincerity into question. And therefore Julius, Bishop of Rome, cited the eastern Bishops to appear before him in a Council to justify not their authority but their integrity. And when they would not appear the Council absolved Athanasius from excommunication, and received him into communion, acknowledging thereby that Athanasius, by the sentence of the Council of Tyre, did really and truly and regularly stand excommunicate from the western churches as well as from the eastern, and by consequence from the Church Catholic until that absolution. And agreeable to this it is that Athanasius, to prove that Arius died out of the pale of the church, represents that he died the night before he was to be received into communion by the Eusebians. For by this story he acknowledges that those who were received into communion by the Eusebians were in communion with the Church Catholic. So then, by the consent of Athanasius, Pope Julius and all their party, the Eusebian Councils before the rupture between the Eastern and Western Churches were authentic, and their Acts valid and binding.

It remains therefore that we inquire whether the Council of Tyre dealt sincerely or corruptly in the cause [case] of Athanasius.

Quest. IV

Whether it was a dead man's hand in a bag, or the dead body of Arsenius which was laid before the Council of Tyre to prove that Arsenius was dead.

Quest. V

Whether it was Arsenius alive or only his letter which Athanasius produced in the Council of Tyre to prove that he was not dead.

Quest. VI

Whether the story of producing the dead man's hand and the living Arsenius in the Council of Tyre, was not feigned by Athanasius about five and twenty years after the time of the Council of Tyre.

These three questions being of a kind I consider together as one. For Historians tell us that when Athanasius was accused of the death of Arsenius he represented that Arsenius was alive, and thereupon the Accusers, to prove that he was dead, produced in the Council of Tyre a dead man's hand in a bag representing that it was the hand of Arsenius cut off by Athanasius for magical uses, and Athanasius confuted them by setting the living Arsenius before the Council and pulling out the man's two hands from under his cloak to let the Council see that neither of his hands were cut off ; at which the accusers of Athanasius were ashamed and the Council proceeded no further in that accusation, there being some among them who knew Arsenius.

And the truth of this story I question, because I find it was unknown in the times next after the Council even to Athanasius himself, as well as to others, till he published it. For Athanasius, about five years after the Council of Tyre, that is, about the year 440, when he was ready to be expelled his bishopric the second time, called a Council at Alexandria of ninety Egyptian Bishops, and in their name wrote a large elaborate letter to all the world in his own defence against the accusations and proceedings in the Council of Tyre, and seems to omit nothing that could be thought of in his behalf, and yet says not one word of the dead man's hand, nor of Arsenius appearing alive at Tyre. Neither is there any mention of these things in the letter which Pope Julius about two years after wrote to the Eastern Bishops from a Council at Rome in behalf of Athanasius who was then amongst them. Neither are they mentioned in the two large letters which Athanasius and the bishops of his party, assembled about five years after out of Egypt and all the West in the Council of Sardica, wrote to the same purpose, the one to the Church of Alexandria the other to all the Churches. In all these letters they talk of Arsenius, and say that he was alive but do not say that he appeared alive at Tyre, though that one thing, had it been true, would have been more to the purpose than all the rest which they say. They do not say that they, or any of them, had seen him alive, or that they had witnesses of his being alive, as they might and surely would have done, had he been seen alive before all the world at Tyre.

But that which makes me most doubt of the story is that I

find it otherwise related by Athanasius and his friends in these very letters of the Councils of Alexandria and Sardica. For in these Letters (which, being recorded by Athanasius himself in his Second Apology as well as writ by him and his friends, are of unquestionable authority) they tell the story as if the accusers produced before the Council not a dead man's hand but a dead body ; and Athanasius produced against them not Arsenius alive but his Letter only, and the accusers were so far from being ashamed that the Council, notwithstanding the Letter, proceeded to condemn Athanasius for the murder.

And first that it was a dead body the Council of Sardica in their Letter to the Church of Alexandria tells expressly in these words : " *They (that is the Council of Tyre) said and lamented that Athanasius had committed murder and killed one Arsenius, a Meletian Bishop ; which thing they bewailed with feigned groans and false tears, and commanded, or desired, the BODY of him that lived, as if he had been dead, to be brought before them. But their fallacies [? falsities] did not lie hid. For all men knew that the man did live and was proved to be alive (viz. by his letter). And yet when these versatile men saw their figments thus confuted (for Arsenius being alive has (by his letter) shown that he was not killed nor dead) they would not thus acquiesce but (afterwards in the reign of Constantius) added new false accusations to the old ones, that they might again involve the man in calumnies.*

So then it was not a magical salted hand but the whole preserved body of a dead man which the accusers of Athanasius laid, or desired to be laid, before the Council. In cases of murder 'tis usual to have dead bodies viewed for passing judgment upon them ; and this was done in the Council that by the features and other marks and wounds and testimony of those who knew Arsenius or had seen his body at the time of the murder and buried it and dug it up again the Council might be satisfied whether he was murdered and how. But it seems, to shame the proceedings of the Council, some juggler (I will not say Sorcerer) has transformed the whole body into a magical hand. And on the contrary, by the same art the

Letter of Arsenius has been transformed into Arsenius himself.
For that Athanasius and his friends had no other evidence of
Arsenius's being alive besides that letter, he and his Bishops
in the Council of Alexandria have plainly acknowledged in
these words. "Athanasius," say they, was accused of killing one
Arsenius and breaking the communion cup. But Arsenius is
alive and (in his Letter) desires your communion, and expects
not other testimonies that he should appear alive, but he
himself confesses that he lives, writing in his own letters to our
fellow Bishop Athanasius whom they assert his murderer. Nor
were the impious ashamed to affirm him the murderer of one
who was in a remote place divided from us by journeys both by
sea and land living in a region at that time unknown to all men.
Yea, they studied to hide him and make him disappear when
he suffered nothing. And, as far as they were able, they
translated him into another world, being ready to kill him that
either by his real feigned murder they might kill Athanasius.
But thanks be to the Divine Providence who suffers nothing
unjust to prosper, but hath before the eyes of all men produced
Arsenius living, and openly detecting their calumny and deceit.
For he does not shun us as his murderers nor hate us as injurious
to him (for he suffers no evil from us), but desires to communicate with us and be of our number, as his Letter shews. And
yet, notwithstanding this, they proceeded against Athanasius
and banished him as a murderer. For it was not the Emperor
Constantine but their calumnies which banished him."—Here
you see Athanasius and his bishops are so far from pretending
that he appeared alive at Tyre that on the contrary they insist
only upon the evidence of his Letter, and represent that no other
evidence was to be expected and, by consequence, had no other,
and magnify evidence so much as if God had thereby produced
Arsenius alive before the eyes of all men, and complain that
notwithstanding this Letter the Council of Tyre proceeded
against Athanasius and banished him as a murderer. This
they wrote five years after the Council of Tyre when things
were fresh in their memory and contrary stories were not yet
invented.

So then this Letter is the whole ground of all the confidence wherewith Athanasius and his friends so constantly reported that Arsenius was alive. And though they tell us sometimes that they knew he was alive, or that he had showed that he was not dead, or that God had produced him living and openly detecting the calumny before the eyes of all men, yet they mean only by his Letter. This evidence they magnify thus extravagantly because they had no other. For had they known where he was, or where any witnesses were who had seen him (as they would have known of multitudes had he been seen by all the world of Tyre), they would have sent for him or the witnesses and had them in readiness at their Councils to satisfy all their party, and made a greater noise about such evidence than about a letter which no upright Court of Judicature would allow for any evidence at all. And yet I cannot find that in all their endeavours to overthrow the Council of Tyre they ever pretended to have so much as one living witness who had seen Arsenius alive. So far are the Egyptian Bishops from saying that any of them or anybody else had seen Arsenius at Tyre, that they insist only on the evidence of his Letter, and say that he expects no other testimonies of his being alive, that is, that he contents himself with having given them that testimony, and therefore they are not to look for any other. So far are they from saying that he in person put the accusers to shame or stopped the proceedings of the Council upon this accusation that on the contrary they say that the Council proceeded against Athanasius, notwithstanding the evidence of the Letter, and banished him as a murderer—which deserves well to be noted. For in this one passage you have the concurrent testimony of both parties against his being seen alive in the Council—that of Athanasius and his Egyptian Bishops in objecting nothing more than the Letter of Arsenius against the proceedings of the Council and that of the Eastern Bishops in proceeding on to condemn Athanasius for the murder. For in doing this they adjudged and declared that Arsenius was murdered, and, by consequence, not seen alive in the Council. Nor did they only adjudge and declare this in the Council but afterwards constantly persisted in it, as you may see in their Letter from the Council of Antioch to Pope Julius, and in that which, in their return from the Council of Sardica, they wrote at Philippopolis to all the world. And, for my part, I can more easily believe what both parties affirmed in that age before newer stories were invented than that the bishops of all the East should condemn Athanasius for murdering a man who appeared alive before them in the midst of the Council and owned himself to be Arsenius, and was known by many there ; and be able to satisfy the Emperor Constantine and the Eastern nations of the justness of such a sentence. For upon Athanasius's appealing from the Council, the Emperor heard the cause [case] over again between Athanasius and the Legates of the Council, and he and the East were satisfied in their proceedings.

So then the story of the dead man's hand and the living Arsenius at Tyre seems to be a fable unknown in those times and therefore invented afterwards. And I suspect Athanasius to be the inventor of it because he tells it first of any man in his Second Apology written in the wilderness at the same time that he broached the story of the death of Arius. For if he knew it to be false (as he did if it were so) then he was not imposed upon by others, but told it to impose upon others, and so is the Author of it.

Quest. VII.

Whether the Letter of Pinnes for proving Arsenius to be alive was not feigned by Athanasius at the same time with the story of the dead man's hand.

In all the times of the controversy about the Council of Tyre I cannot find that Arsenius had been seen alive by any living witnesses. The Councils of Alexandria, Rome, and Sardica knew nothing of any such witnesses. But afterwards, when Athanasius was condemned by all the world and so saw that the Letter of Arsenius would not any longer support the belief that Arsenius was alive, he put about a story amongst his credulous followers as if Arsenius himself in person had been found alive first in Egypt with one Pinnes and then at Tyre, and tells the story of his first finding thus :—

" Now that Arsenius was hidden (by the Meletians) that they might make his murder more probable, his friends who were with him testified. For in seeking him we found one of them who wrote to John (another actor in the same false accusation) the following Letter.

" To the beloved Brother John Pinnes, a Presbyter of the house of Ptemengyris which is in the name of Anteopolis, wisheth health.

I would have you know that Athanasius sent his Deacon into Thebais to search all places for Arsenius. Pecysius the presbyter and Sylvanus the brother of Helias and Tapenacerameus and Paul the Monk of Hypseles, being first found, confessed that Arsenius was with us. But when we had learnt that, we caused him to be put into a ship and carried down with Helias the Monk into the lower parts (of Egypt). And soon after, the Deacon with some others coming upon us went into our house and found him not by reason that we had sent him, as was said, into the lower parts. But me and Helias the Monk who had conveyed him away they carried away with them to Alexandria, and brought us before the governor, and I could not deny but confessed that he lived and was not killed. The same thing was confessed by the Monk who had carried him away. Wherefore, Father, I make known to you these things that you may not accuse Athanasius. For they said that he was alive and hidden with us and it was made known to all Egypt and cannot any longer be concealed. I Paphnutius a Monk of the same house who have written this Epistle salute you much.
Farewell.

Now the truth of this Epistle I suspect for these reasons. First because Athanasius and his friends knew nothing of this evidence in the Councils of Alexandria, Rome, and Sardica. So many living witnesses that Arsenius was alive and the proof thereof by some of those witnesses before the governor of Egypt, would have made a much greater noise in the Council of Tyre and afterwards than the single Letter of Arsenius : and yet Athanasius and his friends at that time insisted only upon the evidence of this Letter representing that Arsenius himself had shewed by his letter that he was alive, and intended no other evidence of his being alive and complaining that the Council of Tyre had banished Athanasius notwithstanding that Letter. This was all that Athanasius and his friends had then to allege, as we have shewed out of the letter of the Council of Alexandria.

And, secondly, I suspect the Letter of Pinnes because it represents things contrary to what Athanasius and his friends did in the Letter of the Council of Alexandria. For here we are told that Arsenius at first lay hid in Upper Egypt till the Deacon of Athanasius upon search discovered him, and that he then retired into the lower Eygpt and soon after, as Athanasius adds, wrote his famous letter. But in the Letter of the Council of Alexandria we are told that the accusers of Athanasius were not ashamed to affirm him the murderer of one who was in a remote place divided from the Egyptians by journeys both by sea and land, living in a region at that time unknown to all men, and being hidden by them and translated as far as could be into another world until he made himself known by his letter.

And lastly the stories of finding Arsenius first in Egypt and then at Tyre are of a kind, and were told by the same man at the same time and therefore stand or fall together.

QUEST. VIII.

Whether the Letter of Arsenius was not feigned by Athanasius before the convening of the Council of Tyre.

This famous letter pretended to be written by Arsenius after he had for some time lain hidden runs thus :—

" To Athanasius the Blessed Pope, Arsenius, Bishop of the City of Hypselita which was formerly under Meletius, and to the Presbyters and Deacons much health in the Lord.

And we, loving peace and union with the Catholic Church which you by the grace of God are set over, and, desiring to be subject to the ecclesiastical canon according to the ancient law do write to you, beloved Pope, promising in the name of the Lord that we will not henceforward communicate with Schismatics and such as are not in peace with the Catholic Church, whether they be Bishops or Presbyters or Deacons ; neither will we assemble ourselves with them in any Synod, nor send them letters of peace nor receive such letters from them, nor, without the advice and assent of you the Metropolitan Bishop, make any decree about Bishops or about any other common ecclesiastical opinion ; but we will give place to the received canons after the manner of Ammonianus, Tyrannus, Phisianus and the other Bishops. Moreover we beseech your humanity therefore to write back to us as soon as may be and also to our fellow Bishops concerning us, and shew them that we now stand to the ancient decrees, being at peace with the Catholic Church and united to the fellow Bishops of those regions. And we believe that by your prayers, as being powerful, this peace will remain firm and indissolvable to the end according to the will of God the Lord of all things, through Jesus Christ our Lord. The whole Clergy that is under you, we and they that are with us, salute, and so soon as God shall permit we will come to your humanity. I Arsenius wish you may long fare well, most blessed Pope."

Now the truth of this letter I suspect, first because it has not the form and humour of a free letter, but looks like some formal covenant of submission drawn up by a Lawyer to be imposed upon Arsenius, or like a recantation imposed on him by a magistrate. Then, because Arsenius, had he been of the mind here expressed, would certainly have made good his promise of coming to Athanasius. He would not have suffered the whole Roman world for many years to continue in war and confusion about his death, but have speedily shown himself to the Emperor and to the world to the confusion of all the enemies of his dear friend Athanasius. Thirdly, because, were this letter genuine, Athanasius must have known how to write back to Arsenius and, consequently, knowing where he was, would have sent and fetched him by fair means or by foul, and shewed him alive to the Emperor. Lastly, because I find this letter directly contradicted by Athanasius himself. For he, in his Apology (ii. p. 783) tells the story of the hand after this manner. "Arsenius," saith he, "was first found hid in Egypt ; afterwards those of our side found him hidden at Tyre. And, which is strange, when he was found, he would not confess himself to be Arsenius until in judgment he was convicted by Paul, Bishop of Tyre. And from that time, being ashamed, he denied himself no more. Now he did that to keep the compact he had made with the Eusebians, lest, he being found and discovered, the plot should be laid open and dissolved." This passage, I say, wherein Arsenius is represented confederate with the Eusebians till the Council of Tyre, does absolutely contradict his letter wherein he is made to renounce that party and side with Athanasius before. Nor can it be pretended that Arsenius turned to and fro : seeing Athanasius with his Bishops in the Council of Alexandria, four or five years after the Council of Tyre, pleaded from this letter that Arsenius desired their communion. So then both these contradictory records cannot be true, or rather, they must both be false, destroying one another. For, had Arsenius been discovered in such a manner at Tyre, then would not Athanasius and his Bishops, a while after in the Council of Alexandria, have collected and pleaded from this letter writ before, that he did at that time desire their communion. And, had the Letter been genuine, Athanasius would not afterwards have overthrown the credit of it by telling that contrary story of Arsenius at Tyre. But it seems his memory failed him.

Quest. IX.

Whether the Letter of Ischyras was not feigned by Athanasius.

When Athanasius was accused of the above mentioned crimes by Ischyras, he pretended that Ischyras became penitent and wrote the following letter :

"To the Blessed Pope Athanasius, Ischyras wisheth health

in the Lord. Seeing, upon my coming to you Lord Bishop to
be received into the Church, you chid me for what I had
heretofore spoken, as if I did that on my own accord, I have,
therefore sent you this Apology in writing that you might
know that there was force done to me, and that I was beaten
by Isaac, and Heraclides, and Isaac of Leotis, and by their
companions. But I, calling God to witness upon this, do say
for my excuse that I am conscious of none of those things done
by you of which they speak. For neither was there any cup
broken nor holy table overthrown, but all these calumnies
they urged me to by force. These things I apologise for
myself, and give you in writing, desiring to be one of your
assembly. Farewell in the Lord. I have given this my hand
to you, Bishop Athanasius, in the presence of the Presbyters
Ammon of Dicelle, Heraclius of Phasco, Boccon of Chenebri,
Achillas of Myrsene, Didymus of Tophosiris, and Justus of
Bomotheus ; and of the Deacons of Alexandria, Paul, Peter
and Olympius, and these of Mareste, Ammonius, Pistus,
Demetrius and Gaius."

Now this Letter I suspect because it looks as if contrived
rather for the interest of Athanasius than that of Ischyras, and
seems more like a formal recantation or certificate than a free
Letter, and also contains a ridiculous story. For it is ridiculous
that men should go about to procure false accusers or witnesses
by forcing or beating them ? And were a false accuser or witness
so procured 'tis not likely that after his discovering the knavery
he would go on in accusing or witnessing as Ischyras did to the
end. Could a beating bout make Ischyras so hearty in the
cause ?

And further, if Ischyras went to Athanasius to be reconciled
to him and received into communion, as this letter represents,
he went with design either to confess his fault or not. If to
confess, how came Athanasius to let him go without taking his
confession before witnesses ? If not to confess, how could he hope
to be pardoned and received by Athanasius? And afterwards,

if he sent this Letter of confession, how came Athanasius then to neglect sending for him and making his advantage of the opportunity ? Would Athanasius send up and down the world to seek Arsenius and not accept of Ischyras when he offered to come in, but content himself with a bare letter ? These things don't consist.

But that which looks most oddly is the witnessing of this Letter. For witnesses are never set to Letters. They are set to no sort of writings but such as are designed for evidence in legal proceedings, and therefore shew that the author of this letter designed it for evidence : that is, he designed by those witnesses to make it evidence for Athanasius against Ischyras. For there was no need of such evidence against anybody else. Were these witnesses added to give credit to this Letter with Athanasius ? There was no need of that. Were they added to give credit to it with others ? Then the design of it was not to make an interest with Athanasius for Ischyras, but to make an interest with others for Athanasius against Ischyras. Had Ischyras been penitent and desired to be reconciled to Athanasius, as this Letter represents, he would not have sent a certificate to Athanasius against himself, but have wrote an insinuating letter in general terms, and have reserved himself to be useful to Athanasius as an evidence, upon condition of pardon and reconciliation ; and no doubt Athanasius would have accepted the condition with both hands.

There is another thing which looks very suspiciously. For many persons are named as witnesses but in such a manner as makes it plain that their hands were not to the letter. Would any man call his friends together to be witnesses to a writing, and not make them set their hands to it ? If Ischyras wrote this Letter he either designed it for evidence or he did not. If he did not, he would have made no mention of witnesses. If he did, he would certainly have caused them to set their hands to it. It looks therefore as written by somebody else who had a mind to give credit to it by witnesses, but knew not how either to procure or conterfeit their hands.

And the suspicion is much increased by considering that the truth of this letter was never proved (that I can find) by the actual testimony of any of the witnesses. The Letter was written before the Council of Tyre, and, by consequence, alleged in that Council and in the Councils of Alexandria, Rome, and Sardica where Athanasius was present ; but no witness that I can read of were ever brought to prove it. Julius, Bishop of Rome, in his letter for Athanasius, tells how Athanasius produced the authentic handwriting of Ischyras confessing that he was suborned. He does not say that Athanasius had proved by witnesses that Ischyras wrote that confession, but lays the whole stress of the evidence upon the handwriting of Ischyras. I would ask, therefore, whether Athanasius and his friends did try to get this Letter proved in the Council of Tyre and on other occasions or not. If they did not, it argues a guilty conscience. For without any examination of the business they took it for granted that the witnesses would be against them, and therefore did not believe the reality of their testimony to the Letter. But if they did try, and upon examining the witnesses found them against this Letter, then is the Letter false by the concurrent testimony of those very witnesses cited to prove it true. And this is to me a very great argument of suspicion. For the case is as if a man should produce a bond wherein 'tis written that the party, pretended to be bound, signed it before such and such witnesses, but whose hands are not to the bond, and before a Judge should produce none of the witnesses, but confess that he never spake with them or that they are all against him, being the Defendant's friends, and only plead that they are good witnesses because in the bond (pretended to be sent in a letter to the Plaintiff) 'tis written that the Defendant signed it in their presence. So impudent a case as this was scarce ever brought before a civil Magistrate.

Quest. X.

Whether the Recantation of Valens and Ursacius was not feigned by the friends of Athanasius.

When Athanasius, being banished first by Constantine the Great and then by his son Constantius, appealed from the Council of Tyre to the Pope, and the Eastern bishops were thereupon summoned first to the Council of Rome and then to the Council of Sardica to appear and plead their cause, but would not subject themselves to the authority of the Pope and the jurisdiction of the Western bishops ; Constans, Emperor of the West, by the impulse of the Western bishops, wrote a letter to his brother Constantius, threatening that if he would not restore Athanasius and animadvert upon his adversaries, he would come himself and restore him by force. Whereupon Constantius, being reduced to great straits, called many of the Eastern bishops together, and they advised him that it was better to let Athanasius have his Church than undertake a civil war. Constantius therefore invited Athanasius back by courteous letters, and a while after Ursacius and Valens, two Bishops of Pannonia who had been principal actors in the condemnation of Athanasius, were said to have written voluntarily two letters, the one from Aquileia to Athanasius wherein they declare that they desire his communion, the other at Rome to the Pope. The Epistles are as follows :

" To our Lord and Brother Athanasius the Bishop
Ursacius and Valens Bishops.

Having our opportunity by our Brother and fellow Presbyter Musoeus, who is going to your humanity, dear brother we salute you much by him from Aquileia, and wish that you may read our epistle in health : whereof you will make us certain, if you please to write back to us. For that we have peace with you and ecclesiastical communion you may know by these our Letters. The Divine Providence preserve you, Dear Brother."

To Our Lord the Blessed Pope Julius
Valens and Ursacius wisheth health.[1]

Since it is manifest that we formerly insinuated by our
Letters many heinous things concerning Athanasius and, being
convened by the letters of your Holiness, could not give an
account of what we had signified, we confess to your Holiness
in the presence of all the Presbyters our brethren that all things
which heretofore came to our ears concerning Athanasius are
false and feigned and of no force. And therefore we most
willingly embrace the communion of the said Athanasius,
especially since your Holiness, according to your innate good-
ness, hath been pleased to pardon our error. We profess also
that if at any time the Oriental Bishops or even Eusebius
himself shall with an evil mind call us into judgment concerning this thing, we will not go thither without your consent.
And the heretic Arius and his followers who say there was a
time when the Son was not and affirm that the Son is of nothing
and deny that he was before all ages, as by our former
confession which we made at Milan, so now and always we
anathematize."

The second of these two epistles is said by Hilary to have
been written before the first upon the occasion of a Council
convening at Sirmium against Photinus two years after the
Council of Milan, and, by consequence, four years after the
Council of Sardica. For Petavius and Valesius agree with
Socrates in placing this Council of Sirmium in the year 351,
and the Council of Sardica met A.C. 347 ; and Liberius in his
Epistle to Constantius, written after George was made Bishop
of Alexandria and by consequence A.C. 356 or A.C. 357, reckons
eight years from the Council of Milan to the writing of that
Epistle, and therefore the Council of Milan was celebrated
A.C. 348 or 349.

Now this second Epistle I suspect for many reasons.

1. It is a confession attested by nameless witnesses and was
never proved.

[1] Apud Athanas. Apol. ii, and Hilary. Fragm.

G

2. The crime is too great and shameful for Bishops to acknowledge voluntarily, as Valens and Ursacius are here represented to have done. Nor is it likely that after such a confession they could have acted in the Western Councils with so great authority, reputation and success as they did.

3. Eusebius, who is mentioned in the Epistle as then living, was dead some years before. And if, with Hilary and Sozomen, to avoid this objection you write *Athanasius* for *Eusebius*, the sense will be hard, for Athanasius will be accused of an evil mind ; which is contrary to the design of the Epistle.

4. The saying that Valens and Ursacius, being required to prove the things charged against Athanasius, could not do it is not consistent with the proceedings in the Council of Sardica. For there five of the six Bishops then living, who had been sent from the Council of Tyre to Mareste [Mareotis] to examine the business of Ischyras (two of which five were Valens and Ursacius) propounded to the Western bishops that an equal number of both parties should be sent again to Mareste to examine things anew, and if the crime did not appear, they five would be excommunicated, but if it did, the like number of the Western bishops who created the disturbance should be excommunicated by the Eastern. But the Western bishops would not accept of equal terms. The Eastern must submit to the authority of the Pope and jurisdiction of the Western or go for criminals.

5. Pope Liberius (vide Hilarii Fragm.), in his letters to Constantius in behalf of Athanasius, makes no mention of this confession of Ursacius and Valens, as he would surely have done had it been newly made to his predecessor.

6. The great Council of Ariminum (vide Hilarii Fragm.), in their Letter to Constantius the Emperor, accused Ursacius and Valens of a Confession made at Milan, saying that after they had been excommunicated upon suspicion of Arianism they begged pardon and were absolved at the Council of Milan before the Legates of the Pope. But of this other Confession

made two years after at Rome, upon occasion of the convening of the Council of Sirmium, they make no mention, though that would have been much more material had it been true.

7. Ursacius and Valens were excommunicated but once, that is to say, in the Council of Sardica, and one excommunication admits of but one absolution. If you place the Council of Milan before the Council of Sardica, the first confession and absolution will be before the Western bishops excommunicated any of the Eastern for Arianism, and the second before Athanasius went from Rome into the East : both of which are plainly absurd, for the second confession was afterwards sent to Athanasius out of the West by Paulinus, bishop of Treves. And further, the Council of Sardica, in their letters whereby they declare Valens and Ursacius excommunicate for Arianism, would have taken notice of their former excommunication, recantation, and absolution—had there been any such thing. But if you place the Council of Milan after the Council of Sardica, as you ought to do, then Valens and Ursacius will recant, and be absolved twice from one excommunication : and, which increases the absurdity, the Bishop of Rome alone will absolve them from what a Council, where he himself was present by his Legates, had absolved them before. For their second recantation plainly respects the proceedings of the Council of Sardica. So, then, there is no place for this second recantation.

Quest. XI.

Whether Athanasius was falsely accused, or did falsely accuse Eusebius of Adultery before the Council of Tyre.

Philostorgius tells us (Philostorg. L.2. c.12) that when Athanasius being impelled by the Emperor's threatening, came to Tyre, he would not submit to stand in judgment, but sent in a big-bellied woman, whom he had hired to accuse Eusebius of Adultery, hoping that by the tumult which would probably be raised, he might escape being tried. But when Eusebius asked her if she knew the man and whether he was amongst the Bishops then present, she answered that she was not so senseless as to accuse such men of base lusts, and by those words discovered [revealed] the fraud. This story the other historians Sozomen and Theodoret (Sozom. L.2. c. 25, Theod. L.1. c. 30) invert as if the whore was hired by the Eusebians to accuse Athanasius and the fraud detected by one of Athanasius's friends to the confusion of his accusers. But this last story was unknown to Athanasius and his friends in the times next after the Council of Tyre. For in the Letters of the Councils of Alexandria, Rome, and Sardica, they mention it not, though they omit nothing which made against that Council : and this story, had it been true, would have made more against it than anything else they say. Nor does Athanasius mention it in all his works. Whence I suspect his friends sometime after the writing of his Apologies inverted the story of the accusation.

QUEST. XII.

Whether Athanasius did sincerely acquit himself of the crime of breaking the communion cup of Ischyras.

When Athanasius became bishop of Alexandria, he was soon accused of tyrannical behaviour towards the Meletians so as with his own hands to break the communion cup of Ischyras, a Meletian Presbyter in Mareotis then performing sacred rites, and to subvert the Altar and cause the Church to be demolished. This was the true accusation, as I find by the letter of the eighty Eastern bishops at Sardica recorded in Hilary's Fragments.

On the other hand, Athanasius and his party represented that Ischyras was no Priest, the place, no church, the day not the Lord's Day ; that Athanasius went not thither himself but only sent Macarius, who found Ischyras not celebrating the sacrament but sick in bed, and charged him not to proceed in those things ; and that Ischyras, so soon as well, fled to the Meletians and Eusebians, who thereupon composed the accusation. But were this representation the truth, there could have been no colour for framing an accusation. For cunning men never venture to frame false accusations without some considerable colour of circumstances handsomely laid together. The mystery therefore I take to be this.

I find by a letter of Constantine the Great to Athanasius that Athanasius and Macarius were both of them accused, and by the letter which the eighty Eastern bishops wrote at Phillipopolis compared with some passages cited by Pope Julius out of the Acts of the Council of Tyre, that when indeed Macarius was sent by Athanasius he found Ischyras was sick in bed, but that Athanasius was accused for coming also himself when Ischyras was administering the Eucharist and for breaking the communion cup and overturning the altar with his own hands.

So then it seems (according to the accusation) Macarius was sent first to forewarn Ischyras of executing the office of a Presbyter ; and afterwards, when he would not desist, Athanasius, coming at a time proper to find him in the act, overthrew the sacred things and caused the place to be demolished, Macarius perhaps assisting him. Now the accusation lying only against this last act, Athanasius, to acquit himself, confounds this time with the former and undertakes to prove (not before the Council of Tyre where the accusation was understood, but amongst the credulous Western bishops and others of his own party) that Macarius went alone without Athanasius and found Ischyras sick in bed in a place which was not a church on a day which was not the Lord's Day and only reproved him without breaking the communion cup and subverting the sacred things, and, by consequence, that the accusation that Athanasius found him on the Lord's Day in a Church administering the Eucharist, and subverted the sacred things was a figment. Now if Athanasius shuffled in making this defence, it is plain that he was gravelled and wanted [lacked] a just defence, which is enough to decide the question.

Quest. XIII.

Whether Athanasius was not made Bishop of Alexandria by sedition and violence against the Canons of that Church.

Sozomen (L.2. c. 25) tells us that in the Council of Tyre Athanasius was accused by all in common that he acquired the Bishopric by the perjury of certain bishops when all the bishops had agreed before that no man should be ordained before they had ended the brawls which were between them. For Eusebius writes[1] that when the Council of Nice was ended there burned an implacable fury of contention among the Egyptians. And Socrates tells us[2] (out of the letters of the bishops written at that time) that this contention was about the Nicene decree of the word " homoousios "; those who disliked it thinking the opinion of Sabellius and Montanus was introduced by those who allowed it, and therefore calling them impious, as if they took away the existence of the Son of God ; and, on the contrary, those who allowed this word thinking that the worship of many Gods was introduced by their adversaries, and therefore shunning them as if they introduced the superstition of the Gentiles.

Upon the death of Alexander, therefore, there being gathered out of Thebais and all Egypt forty and four bishops, as the accusers[3] of Athanasius affirmed, they agreed under oath that no man should be ordained before they had ended these brawls, and then they should elect a new bishop by common consent ; but some of these bishops, violating their oath, ordained Athanasius privately without the consent of the rest, for Athanasius[4] with a part of the people rushing one evening into the Church called Dionysius's and finding there certain bishops, shut the doors and caused the bishops, after much reluctancy, to ordain him. Whereupon the rest of the Bishops anathematised Athanasius, but he, sending letters in the name of the City to the Emperor, procured a confirmation of his

[1] Vit. Const. L.3, c.23.
[2] Socr. L.1, c.23.
[3] Sozom. L.2, c.17, 23.
[4] Philostorg. L.3, c.11.

ordination and thereby silenced his adversaries. This was the accusation as 'tis represented by Sozomen and Philostorgius. And that there was some truth in it is confessed by Athanasius himself and his bishops in the Council of Alexandria collected about fifteen years after the ordination of Athanasius. Their words are these[1]. "They (i.e. the accusers of Athanasius) say that after the death of Alexander the Bishop, when some few made mention of Athanasius, six or seven bishops ordained him secretly in a hidden place. These things they wrote to the Emperor, being not ashamed to write any kind of lie. But we and the whole City and Province are witnesses that all the multitude, and all the people of the Catholic Church (that is, whom they would acknowledge to be Catholic), being assembled, as with one soul and body cried out with great acclamations, desiring that Athanasius might be Bishop of the Church. This they entreated of Christ by public votes, and this they adjured us to do for many days and nights, neither departing from the Church themselves nor suffering us to depart."

Thus you see, while the Council would seem to correct the accusation in point of circumstances, they confess the sedition and violence of the people, and that the imprisoned bishops resisted them many days and nights together before they would ordain him ; and that all the people by whose violence this was done were no more in number than one of the little Churches built before the reign of Constantine the Great for the 12 Parishes of Alexandria was able to hold.

Nor indeed was Athanasius capable of being ordained, for he was but a Deacon, and the Canon, constituted by Mark the Evangelist and constantly observed till that time, was that there should be twelve Presbyters of that Church, and that out of them the Bishop should be always elected.

And besides he was scarce of age for such a dignity, for he was then but a youth scarce twenty-five years old[2]; whence the

[1] Epist. Council. Alexandr. apud Athanas. Apol. 2.
[2] Constantin. Imp. apud Athanas. Apol. 2, p.780.

Meletians used to cry : " O wickedness ! He a Bishop or he a Boy ?

To palliate these things the Athanasians have feigned as if Alexander, upon his death, had recommended Athanasius for his successor, and Athanasius out of modesty then hid himself. But this, as it does not excuse the matter, so it looks like a story of later date. For the above-mentioned Council of Alexandria knew nothing of it, though composed of Athanasius and all his bishops. For Athanasius convinced them in his own defence, and in their Epistle where they seem to omit nothing which made for his advantage and particularly defend his election, there is not a word of this story.

By composing all circumstances it is more to be suspected that Athanasius, in the controversy between the Clergy of Alexandria about the Son of God, inflamed differences, thereby to throw out part of the Clergy and make room for himself and his friends, and when he had thus gotten to be Deacon, the reputation and interest he had got with his friends by that controversy served him to invade the Bishopric. For when the people of his party, shutting up themselves with certain of the bishops in a Church, importuned those bishops for many days together to ordain him, I do not hear that he sided with those bishops against the people.

This at least is certain, that the bishops who ordained him resisted for many days together, and were all that time kept prisoners in a church by the mob of his party till they yielded.

And whereas his adversaries objected that those bishops were forced to ordain him contrary to their oaths, it is observable that he and his bishops in the Council of Alexandria make no answer to that part of the objection.

Quest. XIV.

Whether Athanasius was not justly deposed by the Council of Tyre.

The arguments for the justness of the sentence are very great.

1.   The Council of Tyre was a very full one. So that if some

bishops would have been partial there were others numerous
enough to reduce them to modesty. And if it be objected that
the Council was not free because the Emperor was present
there by his Deputy with guards of soldiers, the objection lies
stronger against the Council of Nice where the Emperor was
present in person, and that with a design to influence the
decision of the Council ; whereas at Tyre his Deputy was
present only to see peace kept. The strange heats at Nice
between the Bishops admonished the Emperor to prevent the
like at Tyre, and if he had not done so there could have been
nothing but confusion ; Athanasius bringing a great multitude
out of Egypt to create disturbance and behaving himself very
turbulantly in his trial,[1] as the Council of Tyre in their circulatory letters complained.

2. It is objected that at the examination of witnesses at
Mariote there was present but one party. The accuser,
Ischyras, say they, was there, but the defendants Athanasius
and Macarius were both absent, nor were any of the Presbyters
of Athanasius allowed to be present at the examinations, though
they desired it. Well, but if the accusers of Athanasius brought
several witnesses to Tyre, as no doubt they did, and after both
parties had been heard face to face the Council had a mind
to give themselves the utmost satisfaction by sending to the place
such persons as they thought fit, some to cite witnesses others to
take depositions, but none to act as Judges or accusers, and if
the Delegates at their return acted the part of witnesses before
the Council, and the Council as Judges heard the evidence of
these witnesses between Athanasius and Ischyras ; is the
Council to be blamed for this ? For that this was the true
case is manifest by the Letter of the Council of Alexandria,
wherein Athanasius and the Egyptian bishops say that[2] the
Delegates of the Council of Tyre were not ashamed of Judges
to become witnesses. Had Athanasius desired that witnesses
might be examined for him as well as against him and that some-

[1] Sozom. c.24.
[2] Epist. Concil. Alex.

body might go on his behalf to cite the witnesses who were for
him, as well as Ischyras went to cite the witnesses against him,
the Council could not in justice have denied such a request.
But he pretended not to have any witnesses ; for he and his
friends never complained that their witnesses were not
examined. All their complaint was that they were not admitted
to except against the witnesses of Ischyras, as being either
heathens or Catechumeni, or Arians, or Meletians, or
Colluthians, or persons suborned (if orthodox) or anything else
than the friends of Athanasius. For Athanasius and his friends
exclaim against the Delegates for examining all those sorts of
people, as if heathens were not as good witnesses in matters of
fact as anybody else. So then whilst Athanasius affirmed there
was no church demolished, no altar overturned, no cup broken,
the day not Sunday, the place no church, and he himself not
there, he could produce no witnesses to prove what he affirmed,
but Ischyras produced many upon the place to prove the
contrary.

The presbyters of Athanasius sent to the Council of Tyre in a
letter by some of their members all the evidence they could,
and that was only their own testimony. This evidence (if men
can give evidence in their own cause) the Council of Tyre had
before them, to compose it with other evidence to the contrary,
and surely knew what stress to lay upon it. So that I see not
what was wanting to enable them to judge righteously.

3. When the Legates returned from Tyre and Athanasius
was fully heard and condemned he fled from Tyre and appealed
to the Emperor Constantine the Great. Whereat the Emperor,
by an angry letter, summoned the Council to come and give an
account of their proceedings. But they sent only six Legates.
And then the Emperor heard all the cause over again between
Athanasius and the Legates, approved the proceedings of the
Council and banished Athanasius. Tis true that Athanasius
represents that the Legates feigned a new calumny against him,
whereby the Emperor, being incensed, banished him in a passion

without hearing the cases of Arsenius and Ischyras ; but the eighty Eastern bishops in the Letter which in their return from Sardica, they wrote at Philippopolis to the Churches, say the contrary. For, relating how six bishops who were sent to Mareotis returned to Tyre and confirmed the truth of their accusations, they add " Unde in presentem Athanasium dignam pro criminibus sententiam (Patres) dicunt. Propter quod Tyro fugiens Imperatorem appellat. Audit etiam Imperator, quique interrogatione habita omnia ejus flagitia recognoscens, sua illum sententia in exilium deportavit."

4. Five years after was the Council of Alexandria of eighty Bishops called by Athanasius against the Council of Tyre ; but whilst they examined not the cause between Athanasius and his accusers, nor sent to Mareotis to examine witnesses, but relied on the feigned Letters of Arsenius and Ischyras and such other reports as Athanasius and some presbyters of his party had spread abroad, but never proved, and whilst Athanasius himself (the party accused and condemned) presided in the Council, and most probably penned their letter : what they did can amount to nothing more than prejudice.

Neither did the Councils of Rome and Sardica examine the cause between Athanasius and his accusers, or send to Mareotis to inform themselves, but relied upon the credit of the Council of Alexandria and that of the presbyters of Athanasius, and were also influenced by ambition, their design being to make the Pope universal Bishop, and under him to exercise jurisdiction over the Eastern Churches. For the Pope summoned the bishops of those churches to the Council of Rome to be judged, and when they checked him for his ambition, and refused to come and subject themselves, the Council of Rome absolved Athanasius without any judicial process, as if the Eastern bishops, by not subjecting themselves and coming to plead, had acknowledged themselves guilty. Afterwards the Council of Sardica proceeded upon the same ground, excommunicating the chief of the Eastern bishops because they would not come to submit themselves, and making a Decree that Appeals might be made from all the world to the Pope. This intermixing of the concern for the Universal Bishopric puts a prejudice upon the proceedings for Athanasius, and makes them irregular and void. And the prejudice is increased by the case of Marcellus who was deposed by the Eastern bishops for heresy and absolved and justified by the Councils of Rome and Sardica, and yet afterwards acknowledged by all the world to be guilty of the heresy for which he was deposed. Now if the Councils of Alexandria and Rome neither acted judicially nor without prejudice, then has there been nothing done to dissolve the judgment of the Council of Tyre, and therefore that Council is still in force.

5. The proceedings against Athanasius are further cleared by a proposal made at the Council of Sardica by five of the six bishops who were sent from Tyre to Mareotis, namely that an equal number of bishops should be sent by both parties to the places where Athanasius had committed his crimes to examine things anew, and if the report which those five had made to the Council of Tyre appeared to be false they would stand excommunicated without complaining to anybody; but if it were found true, then five of those bishops who abetted Athanasius should be excommunicated and complain to nobody. But this equal condition the friends of Athanasius durst not accept of.

6. About six years after the Council of Sardica, viz. A.C. 353 Constantius, being now Emperor of both East and West, called a Council at Arles in Gallia to have the condemnation of Athanasius subscribed, and for that end[1] by a courteous letter sent by Montanus invited Athanasius to his presence[2], designing that his cause should be heard anew before this Council for the satisfaction of the Western Bishops. But Athanasius declined[3]

[1] Athanas. Apol. i.
[2] Constant. Epist. ad Aegyptios apud Athanas. Apol. i.
[3] Sozom. L.4, c.9.

the judgment as he had done that of the Council of Caesarea before in the reign of Constantine the Great. In this Council[1] the Pope's Legates, Vincentius of Capua and Marcellus, proposed that for the peace of the Churches they were ready to subscribe the condemnation of Athanasius provided the heresy of Arius might be first condemned. But being told it belonged not to them to prescribe the order of things or to go upon other business than what the Emperor had convened them for, all the Council subscribed except Paulinus of Treves who was therefore banished. And thereupon Pope Liberius,[2] in an Epistle to Hosius, complained that he believed that the Gospel of God might have been preserved by his Legate Vincentius, but yet he not only failed of obtaining the proposals he was to insist on, but was brought over to subscribe. Two years after this another Council was called at Milan of 300 Bishops, and Diogenes[3] was sent to bring Athanasius by force, but, being resisted by the people, returned without him. In this Council therefore the bishops all subscribed readily except Lucifer Calaritanus, the Pope's Legate and Eusebius Vercellensis. Eusebius[4] laid down before the Council the Nicene creed, promising to do what they required if that were first subscribed, but when the sentence of[5] Athanasius was insisted on as the business of the Council, he persuaded Dionysius of Milan that the Nicene faith was struck at, and fraudulently procured his name to be wiped out of the subscriptions. Whereupon these three were banished.

In the beginning of the next year Syrianus, being sent with an armed force to take Athanasius and place George in his room, after he had staid awhile at Alexandria attempted to take him, and the same year a Council was called at Bituris in Gallia. But Athanasius after some resistance escaped, and the bishops now convened subscribed his condemnation, except Hilary

[1] Epist. Liberii Papae apud Lucif. Calar in fin. et. Bibl. Sand.
[2] Apud Baron. an.353, s.19.
[3] Athan. Apol. i. Sozom. L.4, c.9. Baron. an.354, s.17.
[4] Hilar. ad Constantium.
[5] Maximus apud Ambros. serm. 69 de natali Eusebii.

and Rhodanius[1] who promised to subscribe if the Nicene faith
were first ratified ; but for refusing otherwise to subscribe they
were banished. The next year Hosius subscribed at Sirmium,
but Liberius, Bishop of Rome suffered two years banishment,
and then sent a Letter[2] of submission to the Oriental bishops
in which he writes thus :—" Ego Athanasium non defendo,
sed quia susceperat illum bonae memoriae Julius Episcopus
decessor meus, verebar ne forte ab aliquo praevaricator
judicarer. At ubi cognovi quando Deus placuit juxta vos
illum condemnasse, mox consensum meum commodavi sen-
tentiis vestris. . . ." So then Athanasius was now condemned
by all the West except six bishops, and even those, in not
insisting at all upon his innocence, but only objecting[3] the
danger of the faith and proposing to condemn him provided the
Nicene faith might be first confirmed, did really condemn him.
For this was as much as to say that they believed him guilty,
but did not think it safe to subscribe his condemnation before
the Nicene faith was confirmed. So than all the West, as well
as the six bishops who were banished, as all the rest did freely
condemn him in their judgments even before they consented to
subscribe his condemnation. By making this proposal they all
sufficiently confessed that they had not seen Arsenius alive nor
could prove that he had been seen alive, either at Tyre or
anywhere else nor that the Mareotic Acts were false. By this
they declined insisting upon the innocence of Athanasius, and
discovered [revealed] that they durst not rely upon it. By this
they confessed that they had formerly defended him upon other
considerations than his innocence, and that in their consciences
they were satisfied that they might justly, and according to the
Ecclesiastical Canons, subscribe to his condemnation though
not safely till those other considerations were removed.

7.   And if it was not enough for Athanasius to be thus condemned by all the world, it may be considered whether he was

[1] Severus Hist. L.2.
[2] Extat in Hilar. fragm.
[3] Sozom. L.4, c.9 ; Sever. L.2, c.55.

not also condemned by himself. For if the Council of Caesarea was convened by Constantine the Great to hear his cause, and he would not go thither though commanded by the Emperor— and the Council waited long for his coming— ; if the next year, being threatened by the Emperor, he came to the Council of Tyre unwillingly, and brought with him a great multitude to create disturbances that judgment might not proceed ; if when he came there he refused to stand in judgment (all which the Council of Tyre represented[1] in their circulatory Letters), if in like manner he refused to appear at the bar of the Western Councils, and when the Emperor sent an armed power to bring him he resisted that power and fled, and if also both before and after judgment he feigned several stories and letters to justify himself ; and if flying from justice and feigning false excuses be arguments of a guilty conscience, we must allow that Athanasius by doing these things has betrayed himself guilty. The very feigning of letters and stories undermines and overthrows all that was ever said or done for his justification either by himself or others, for it resolves all his defence into a figment ; and such a defence, when detected, is equipollent to a confession of guilt.

QUEST. XV.

Whether Athanasius was not seditious.

The Council of Tyre, in their circulatory Letter wherein they declared his condemnation, charged him with turbulent behaviour in the Council. Constantine the Great, when Antony moved in his behalf, replied that he was petulant, arrogant, and the author of discord and sedition. The Council of Philippopolis represented (as you may see at large in their letter to the Churches) that after his return from Gallia he was more turbulent and tyrannical than before, creating and setting up bishops against bishops in the Eastern churches where he had no authority to intermeddle, and being as exorbitant in Egypt.

[1] Sozom. L.2, c.24.

When he was ready to be banished by the Emperor a second time, he called the Council of Alexandria, and together with them wrote a letter to all the world, in the end of which letter they laboured to part all their friends into a tumult against the Eastern churches, and, by consequence, against their Emperor. For, after a long complaint against the Eastern churches, they thus conclude with an exhortation to invade and destroy them by open force and violence. "Therefore," say they, " how these things are not to go unrevenged even you, beloved, may see. For they are grievous and remote from the doctrine of Christ. For this cause therefore, we, being assembled together, have written in common to you, praying your prudence in Christ to receive this our new contestation and to grieve together with our fellow Bishop Athanasius, and to conceive indignation against the Eusebians, who endeavour these things, that wickedness and malice may not prevail against the Church. For we pray and implore you to be revengers of this injustice, citing the saying of the Apostle, ' Put away from amongst yourselves that wicked person ' (1 Cor. 5. 13). For the things which they do are wicked and not worthy of communion. Therefore hear them not if they write any more against Athanasius : for whatsoever comes from them is false, even though they set the hands of the Egyptian Bishops to their Epistles. For those bishops are not as but Meletians."

This was the carriage of Athanasius and his creatures towards their Emperor and his churches ; and, this being certain record you may thence know of what spirit they were and judge of their carriage in all the rest.

A while after, when their Emperor sent an armed force to displace Athanasius and place Gregory [George] in his room (for Athanasius and his party would never yield to anything but force) he shut himself up in a church with a multitude against the soldiers, and when they could defend the church no longer left it on fire, of which action the Council of Philippopolis make this mention :

" Constituto jam in Athanasii locum ex judicio Concilii sancto et integro sacerdote ut barbarus hostis, ut pestis sacrilega, adductis gentium populis Dei templum incendit, altare comminxit, et clam exit de civitate occultaque profugit." True, Athanasius laid the crime upon the friends of Gregory, but whether the Gregorians burnt a church and defaced an altar they were to use themselves and must repair, or the Athanasians defaced and burnt what they could use no longer, I leave to the reader's judgment.

When Athanasius was thus displaced, he wrote a circulatory Letter to all his friends to stir them up to sedition and revenge. The letter begins thus :—

" The Epistle of Athanasius to the Orthodox of all regions when he suffered a persecution by the Arians.

The things we have suffered are grievous and intolerable and cannot be sufficiently declared : but yet that I may in brief express their grievousness, it is proper to remind you of a history out of sacred writ. A Levite, being injured in his wife and reflecting upon the greatness of the indignity, sent her body cut in pieces to all the Tribes of Israel, that they might look upon this common injury as done not only to him but to them, and that either, if they compassionated his case they might revenge it, or else, if they neglected the wickedness they might be ashamed. Now the messengers told the fact, and they that heard and saw it said there was never any such thing done since Israel came out of Egypt. Therefore all the Tribes were moved, and all of them, as if each had suffered, were gathered together. In conclusion, they that had committed this wickedness were invaded and conquered, and made an anathema by all for they that came together respected not the kindred of the transgressors but the wickedness. You know the story, brethren, and what is reported in the scriptures concerning it, and I will say no more of it seeing I write to them that know it, and am earnest to show you things which transcend these. For I have told you this history that by comparing those things with the present and understanding how these things exceed

H

the cruelty of those, you may conceive a greater indignation than they did against the transgressors. For the bitterness of the persecutions against us is transcendent, and the calamity of the Levite is but small if compared with what is now attempted against the Church . . . "

Then after many things spoken about his expulsion to inflame the Western Churches, he thus goes on :—

" This tragedy," saith he, " Eusebius with his companions long since designed, and now has put them in execution by means of calumnies by which they have traduced us to the Emperor. Nor are they content with this, but seek to kill me, and show themselves so terrible to my friends that they all fly and expect to be slain by them. But ye ought not to conceive fear from their wickedness but rather to revenge it, and be incensed against these innovators. For if when one member suffers all the members suffer, and according to the blessed Apostle we must weep with those that weep ; certainly so great a Church being hurt, everyone ought to revenge the injury as if he himself were hurt. For it is our common Saviour who is blasphemed by them, and they are the Canons of us all which they violate. For if you sat in the Church and the people assembled without any complaint, and suddenly by the Edict of the Prince a successor should be sent to any of you, and such things should be done against you, would you not be, moved with indignation ? would you not seek to revenge it? It is therefore just that you should conceive indignation lest, if this thing be passed by in silence, the mischief creep by degrees into every church and the discipline at length be bought and sold. . . . " Thus far Athanasius.

And this is enough to let you see the spirit of the man. For this shews plainly how, for the sake of a bishopric, he laboured to set the whole Roman world in a flame, and to make a civil war against his own Emperor. For this end, therefore, he fled from Alexandria to Rome, and ceased not to incense the Western bishops till, by their interest with the Western Emperor

Constans, he procured a Council to be called at Sardica wherein it was designed that the Eastern bishops should stand at the Bar as criminals and be judged by the Western in order to their subversion. And when this usurpation would not be yielded unto but ended in that schism between the East and West which Athanasius and his Alexandrine Council solicited, he ceased not till by the same interest the Emperor Constans was prevailed with to threaten a civil war upon his brother Constantius unless he would restore Athanasius.

Thus did this Egyptian Levite go on to revenge the loss of his dear spouse the bishopric of Alexandria, but the Eastern bishops, being men of a more Christian temper, advised their Emperor to peace, and so Athanasius was again restored to the mistress of his affections.

One would think he was now sufficiently revenged of his Emperor, and yet this great spirit stopped not here, but afterwards solicited the Tyrant Magnentius by a letter, which letter after the ruin and death of that Tyrant was found amongst his papers. Athanasius, indeed, in his first Apology saith this Letter was not written by him but feigned by them that found it ; but he that could feign other men's letters could deny his own. In this Apology he answers three objections :—the first, that he had stirred up the Western Emperor Constans against his own Emperor Constantius, the second, that he had endeavoured also by that letter to stir up Magnentius against him, and the third, that he did not afterwards come into the West when the Emperor sent for him, but resisted the messengers. All these things were seditious in a very high degree, and he endeavours to acquit himself of them by answering to the first that he did not stir up Constans, to the second that he did not write that Letter, and to the third that he did not know it was the Emperor's will that he should come into the West, the first of three messengers who were sent for him delivering (as he represents) a lying letter from the Emperor, the next delivering none at all. This was his insincere way of answering.

Whatever he pretends, I must believe that he who wrote two
public circulatory letters to stir up the Western Empire against
the Eastern did endeavour also privately to stir it up, and that
as well in the reign of Magnentius as in that of Constans. For
they who found his letter to Magnentius amongst the papers
of that Tyrant were good witnesses against him, and his denial
of the fact amounts to no more than a prisoner's pleading not
guilty to invalidate the evidence of good witnesses. I must
believe also that he who refused to obey Constantine the Great
was as refractory to Constantius, as Sozomen tells us he really
was (L.4, c.9). For to me it seems incredible that Constantius
should assemble two Councils in the West to hear his cause and
send for him thrice, first by a messenger with a letter, and then
by two other successive messengers with armed forces and he
resist those forces—and yet not understand all this while that
he was sent for. The relation of Sozomen therefore I rather
take to be true, which was as follows :—

" When the first Messenger (Montanus) brought the
Emperor's letters, Athanasius and his friends were extremely
troubled, thinking it not safe for him to go nor without danger
for him to stay. But the advice for his staying prevailed, and so
the messenger returned without doing his business. The next
summer (or rather, as Athanasius saith, after 26 months),
another messenger (Diogenes), being sent from the Emperor
and coming with the Rectors of the province, forced Athanasius
from the city and made a sharp war upon his clergy. But when
the people of Alexandria resumed courage, this messenger also,
seeing the people prepared to fight, returned without com-
passing his message. Not long after the Roman legions were
called out of Egypt and Libya (to Alexandria by Syrianus the
chief commander) and it being told that Athanasius was hid
in the church called Theon, Syrianus and Hilary, who was sent
to hasten this business, taking the soldiers, brake into the
church suddenly at an unexpected time of the night to seek for
Athanasius, but found him not." Thus far Sozomen.

Athanasius represents that he and his people were passing

the night together in devotion, but, by a letter which they wrote four days after (viz. the last day of January) to all the people under Athanasius to stir them up to their assistance, I find that they resisted the soldiers, and by consequence were armed to guard their bishop, and that they kept the church by force, and there hung up the arms of the vanquished soldiers in triumph ; which is a notable instance of the seditious spirit of Athanasius and his followers. The letter is in the works of Athanasius, p. 866, and begins thus :—

" The people of Alexandria to the Catholic Church which is under Athanasius the most reverend Bishop.

We have long since protested concerning the nocturnal invasion which both we and the Church (or Temple) suffered, although there needs no testimony of what the whole city knows. For the bodies of the dead found afterwards were exposed to the people, and the arms and bows which were found in the church do proclaim aloud their wicked fact. Then for stirring up the people to join with them, they represent that the President Syrianus did it without the Emperor's order and was afraid for what he had done, and endeavoured by force to compel them to deny that there was any tumult or anybody slain by the soldiers, and afterwards go on to tell the story thus. " On the fifth of the Kalends of February, we were watching (all night) in the Church and being at prayer because of the assembly that was to meet on the preparation, the Commander Syrianus with many legions of soldiers, having drawn swords and other weapons, and being armed with helmets and other armour suddenly set upon us whilst we were at prayers and reading the scriptures, broke the doors, and some began to throw darts, others cried an All-arm, so that there was made a great clashing of arms, the drawn swords shining by candle light and Virgins were slain and trodden under foot. And whilst their leader marshalled his army, the Bishop sat in his throne and exhorted all to prayers, and, being thrust hither and thither, was almost pulled to pieces ; and when in a great deliquium he lay for dead and now does not appear, we know not what is become of him." A little after they further add that " the arms which were left in the church by those who brake in, and which still hang up in the Church, were no light argument of that hostile incursion so that they could not deny it." " For Gorgonius, the Governor of the City," say they, " often sent a military hangman with a Captain to take them down, but we would not suffer them, that the thing may be known unto all men." Then they go on to say how that as they had already resisted unto blood, so, if it were the Emperor's pleasure that they should be thus persecuted, they were all ready to suffer martyrdom, that is, to die in that resistance. Their words run thus :—" If it be the edict of the Prince to persecute us, we are all ready to suffer martyrdom. But if it be not the Emperor's edict, we entreat the Prefect of Egypt, Maximus, and the other Magistrates that they desire the Prince that such things be no more committed, and we desire that this our prayer may come to him that no other bishop be introduced here. In hindering which we have resisted unto blood, desiring the most reverend Athanasius."

The City being thus inflamed by these incendiaries, there followed other broils before it could be quieted, of all which Lucifer Calaritanus, in a railing book which he wrote against his Emperor Constantius, makes this mention[1] " Recordari, Constanti, de scelerum tuorum memoria recenti quam tibi in Civitate Alexandrinorum inussisti : quantos per abrupta, una tincta subscriptionis tuae dejecerit, quantos gladio demeti fecerit, quantos fami sitique exedi vel carceribus necari, quantos intercepto effecerit spiritu strangulari : et tamen his omnibus crudelitatibus in sanctos martyres quos tuus interfecit gladiatorius animus, cum saeviens ; in nos crudelius saevis dum retines gladium."

Nor were these stirs of short continuance. For Athanasius, exclaiming against the proceedings of Constantius as a vehement persecution and celebrating all those who were slain or taken prisoners as martyrs and Confessors, played the trumpeter to

[1] Lucifer. De Moriend. pro Dei filio.

the rebellion, and kept it up for a good while, as you may understand by that railing book which Hilary wrote against Constantius, in which he has this passage :—" Adest mecum Alexandria tot concussa bellis, tantum commotarum expeditionum expavens tumultum. Brevius enim adversum Persam quam adversum eam armis certatum est. Mutati Prefecti, electi Duces, corrupti populi, commotae Legiones ne ab Athanasio Christus praedicaretur." These words sufficiently shew that the sedition was both great and lasting. So great was it that Constantius, whilst it was on foot, wrote thus to the citizens of Alexandria[1] :—" I know not," saith he, " whether anything ever happened which may be compared with these things, seeing many in this City were blinded, and there presided a man who was emersed from the lowermost Hell ; who as in the dark seduced the desirers of truth to lies . . . and the commonwealth was carried as with a torrent, all things as in a flood being contemned ; and one ruled the multitude who differed nothing from the vulgar mechanics, having contention with the city only because he could not cast it into hell. But that excellent man durst not come to plead his cause in judgment." And in the end of the Letter :—" Whilst the most wretched Athanasius, convicted of most foul crimes, for which he can never be sufficiently punished—no, not though he should be ten times killed—wanders abroad from place to place, it would be absurd to suffer his flatterers and ministers—a sort of jugglers and such as it is not fit to name, to raise seditions here, concerning whom I have long since commanded the Judges to put them to death : who perhaps may not so perish if in time they return from their former crimes (of raising seditions) and shun those to whom the most wicked Athanasius was leader, who hurt the Commonwealth and laid his most impious and wicked hands upon most holy men."

In short, the Egyptians were so seditious that afterwards when Valens would have expelled Athanasius, he could not effect it but found it necessary to desist. For it was not

[1] Exstat Epistola apud Athanasium.

Alexandria alone but all Egypt and Libya which was inflamed
by this sedition, the people with their bishops and presbyters
being everywhere stirred up by the above mentioned Letter
of the Alexandrians, and getting into bodies in the field.
Whereupon at length followed a skirmish in the wilderness like
that nocturnal one at Alexandria, as Athanasius in his first
Apology[1] thus mentions :—" Whilst I was wondering," saith
he, at these things, behold there came again another grievous
report concerning Egypt and Libya, namely that almost ninety
bishops were expelled and their churches given to the Arians ;
sixteen of them being banished and the rest being partly put to
flight and partly compelled to dissemble. For the persecution
there was said to be like that at Alexandria, the brethren being
gathered together in a desert place near a Cemetery to pray on
the Passover and on Sundays, and the Commander of the forces
coming with more than three thousand soldiers armed with
armour and naked swords and arrows, and falling upon the
Christians ; whereupon followed such slaughters as use to
follow in such assaults, the impression being made upon women
and children who did nothing else but pray."

Thus does Athanasius palliate and sanctify these seditions, as
if his party were assembled out of all Egypt and Libya with so
many bishops, and kept the field in a great body together for
no other end but to pray on Sundays, and as if the Roman
Legions came armed to conquer nothing but women and
children. But this is his poetical way of talking in all his
writings.

QUEST. XVI.

Whether Constantius persecuted the Athanasians for religion
or only punished them for immorality.

What sort of Martyrs and Confessors those were whom
Athanasius so much celebrates in his works, you have already
heard, and may further understand by what Athanasius says
of them in his epistle to the Monks, where, speaking first of the

[1] Athanas. Apol. i.

bishops who were banished before the above-mentioned skirmish in the wilderness and then of the bishops of all Egypt, Libya and Pentapolis who in that skirmish were partly put to flight and partly taken prisoners and those banished who would not submit, he saith : [1] " Be it that against Athanasius and the other bishops whom they have banished they could feign false pretences of crimes, yet those things are nothing to this new kind of evil. For what crime could they feign against all Egypt, Libya, and Pentapolis ? For they have not attempted them severally, that they might be able to feign false accusations, but have set upon all together, so that if they should feign anything they should presently be condemned for liars."

To the same purpose Athanasius has another passage in this Epistle : [2] " Be it," saith he, " that they have made Athanasius a criminal, yet what have the other bishops done ? What pretences of crimes have they against them ? What Arsenius was killed by them ? or what Macarius or broken cup are they concerned in ? Or what Meletian acts a part ? Therefore by the things laid to their charge those objected against Athanasius are shewed to be false ; and, mutually, by what has been framed against Athanasius, it is manifest that the things against them are feigned."

These passages sufficiently shew that the best of Athanasius's martyrs and confessors suffered as evildoers and seditious persons, and that Constantius and his bishops studiously avoided punishing them for their faith, and that rather than do it they chose to feign false accusations—if you will believe Athanasius.

Now by the Egyptian martyrs and confessors you may know what these were in other places : of all which Lucifer Calaritanus gives you the following account in speaking thus to Constantius : [3] " Mactasti quamplurimos in Alexandria, laniasti certos toto in orbe, disperdisti resistantes tibi variis in

[1] Athanas. Epist. ad solitariam vitam agentes. p. 857.
[2] *Ibid.*, p. 811.
[3] Lucif. Lib. Moriend. pro filio Dei.

locis. Sed hi omnes, quod tu audire minime vis, martyres sunt ; illos omnes beatissimos tuo mactatos gladio in paradiso esse credimus."

Thus you see the martyrs of the Athanasians, for whom Constantius is in history recorded a persecutor, were such as perished by the sword in resisting the higher powers.

To these you may add the six or seven bishops who were banished for not subscribing the condemnation of Athanasius. For they were deposed by Councils of their own religion, and therefore suffered not for their faith. They endeavoured to keep up a schism between the Eastern and Western Churches, and so were banished as enemies to peace. They refused to debate upon those matters for which the Emperor called the Councils unless they might have their own matters first dispatched, and so suffered as politicians for usurping upon the Emperor's right. They profferred to comply if the Nicene Creed were first ratified, and so acknowledged it lawful to comply, and, by consequence, were banished for resisting the higher powers where it was their duty to obey.

So soon as the Councils of Ariminum and Seleucia were over, Athanasius and his friends, falling into a rage at the Emperor's success, began to write railing books against him ; and Athanasius, indeed, laboured to persuade the Egyptians that the Emperor overcame the Western bishops by tyrannical asperity and terror ; and yet the contrary is certainly true. For Hilary, in a railing book[1] which he wrote at that very time against the Emperor, attributes the success to his clemency. He calls this book a confession, and wishes that he had wrote it in the reign of Nero or Diocletian that he might have suffered for it. For, saith he, " I could have endured any death, whether to be sawn in pieces with Isaiah, or burnt with the three children, or crucified, or cast into the sea " : and then he goes on in these words :

" Adversus enim absolutos hostes felix mihi illud certamen fuisset, quia nec dubium relinqueretur quin persecutores essent

[1] Hilar. cont. Constantium, p. 323., edit. Paris, 1632.

qui ad negandum te poenis, femo, igni compellerent neque ad
testificandum plus tibi nos quam mortes nostras liceret impen-
dere. Pugnaremus enim in palam, et cum fiducia contra
negantes, contra torquentes, contra jugulantes ; et nos populi
tui tanquam duces suos ad confessionis religionem intelligentia
persecutionis publica comitarentur. At nunc pugnamus contra
persecutorem fallentem, contra hostem blandientem, contra
Constantium Antechristum, qui non dorsa caedit sed ventrem
palpat ; non proscribit ad vitam sed ditat ad mortem : non
trudit carcere ad libertatem sed intra palatium honorat ad
servitutem : non latera vexat sed cor occupat non caput gladio
desecat, sed animam auro occidit : non contendit ne vincatur,
sed adulatur ut dominetur. Christum confitetur ut neget ;
unitatem procurat ne pax sit ; haereses comprimit ne Christiani
sint ; Ecclesiae tecta struit ut fidem destruat."

All which is as much as to say that Constantius persecuted
not the men but the faith, and did it not by torture, proscrip-
tions, prisons, and deaths, but by deceiving, flattering, tickling,
enriching, and honouring the Western clergy, and building their
churches. And to the same purpose he adds a little after
(p. 325) :

" Omnia saevissima sine invidia gloriosarum mortium peragis.
Novo inauditoque ingenii triumpho de diabolo vincis et sine
martyrio persequeris. Plus crudelitati vestrae Nero, Deci,
Maximiane debemus : Diabolum enim per vos vicimus. At
tu omnium crudelitatum crudelissime damno majore in nos et
venia minore desaevis. Subrepis nomine blandientis, occidis
specie religionis, impietatem peragis, Christi fidem Christi
mendax praedicator extinguis. Non relinquis saltem miseris
excusationes, ut aeterno judici suo poenas et aliquas laniatorum
corporum praeferant cicatrices : ut infirmitas defendat necessi-
tatem. Scelectissime mortalium omnia ita temperas ut excludas
et in precato veniam et in confessione martyrium. Sed haec
ille pater tuus artifex humanarum mortium docuit, vincere
sine contumacia, jugulare sine gladio, persequi sine infamia,
odire sine suspicione, mentiri sine intelligentia, profiteri sine

fide, blandiri sine bonitate, agere quid velis nec manifestare quae velis."

Thus does Hilary in one and the same breath rail at Constantius as the most cruel of persecutors, and yet declare that his [persecution] consisted in nothing but love and kindness. By this means he had better success than the heathen persecutors by violence, and therefore was, in Hilary's opinion, more cruel, not to the bodies but to the souls of men. Hilary, therefore, finding himself deserted by almost all the world and being thereby reduced to despair, wrote this railing book, and, to provoke the Emperor to kill him, presented it to him at Constantinople A.C. 360 (as Baronius shows[1]) hoping thereby to fix the name of persecutor upon him and that of martyr upon himself. But although this raillery was crimen laesae majestatis, and in that government punishable with death ; yet the Emperor was so far from being provoked to do anything which might but look like persecution that, on the contrary, he thereupon released Hilary out of banishment, and licensed him to return home into Gallia, thus endeavouring to overcome evil with good.

How far this Emperor was from being a persecutor is further manifested by a story told of him by Gregory Nazianzen[2] . . .

The same Gregory Nazianzen also in his first Oration against Julian thus expostulates with the soul of the deceased Constantius for making Julian emperor.

" Quid tibi accedit, O Imperatorum divinissime Christique amantissime (eo enim provehor ut tecum velut cum praesente atque audiente expostulem, etsi multo praestantiorem te esse scio quam ut a me reprehendi debeas, utpote qui Deo adjunctus sis coelestisque gloriae hereditatem acceperis atque in tantum a nobis migravis ut imperium cum meliore commutares) quodnam hoc consilium suscepisti qui omnes non tuae solum sed etiam superioris memoriae Imperatoris anima solertia et acumine longe antecellebas ? "

[1] Baron. An. 360, sect. 8, 9.
[2] Greg. Naz. Carm. Iamb., 21, p. 23.

And a little after excusing Constantius for doing this, he saith, " Cum benignitatem dixi id aperte dixi quod eum crimine omni ac culpa liberet. Cui enim vel ex iis quibus non perinde cognitus erat, dubium est quin ipse ob pietatem amoremque erga nos ac propensissimam bene de nobis merendi voluntatem non modo illum (sc. Julianum) aut totius generis honorem imperiique incrementum neglexisset, verum imperio quoque ipsi omnibusque fortunis, atque ipsi denique vitae qua nemini quicquam est clarius, incollumitatem nostram ac salutem haud illi benti animo praetulisset. Neque enim usquam unquam ullius rei tam acri amore atque cupiditate correptus est, quam ille Christianos crescere atque in summam gloriae potentiaeque amplitudinem pervenire cupiebat. Ac neque domitae et subactae gentes nec respublica praeclaris legibus constituta ac gubernata nec pecuniarum copia, nec gloriae magnitudo, nec quod rex regum et esset et appellaretur, nec omnia alia quibus hominum felicitas declaratur, nec denique quicquam ex omnibus rebus tantum ipsi voluptatis afferebat, quantum ut et nos per ipsum et per nos ipse tum apud Deum tum apud homines floreremus ac firma semper et stabilis nobis potentia permanerat. Qui quidem et siquid nobis molestiae exhibuit, non nostri contemptu id fecit nec ut nos contumelia afficeret aut quod aliis quibusdam potius quam nobis commendare cuperet : sed ut omnes in unum coiremus, animorumque consensione jungeremur nec per schismata inter nos dirempti atque dissecti essemus."

Thus far Gregory. And this testimony, coming freely from the mouth of an enemy and an eye-witness of things is as great as can be desired.

So Libanius, a heathen and therefore another enemy, gives him the same character. For in his Oration called Basiliscus, after he had described the behaviour of Constantius in war, he goes on thus :—

" Verum cum adeo illustris esset in armis, lange praestantior aliis in rebus quam in bellicis fuit ; ut de eo ennuncione liceat, Rex probus hic, bellator et acer. Non enim eo se tum meliorem quam alii visum iri autumabat cum magis quam caeteri saeviret, sed si magis quam clementia gavisus, omnes nihilo secius superaret . . ."

In short, the virtues of this Emperor were so illustrious that I do not find a better character given of any Prince for clemency, temperance, chastity, contempt of popular fame, affection to Christianity, justice, prudence, princely carriage and good government than is given to him even by his very enemies. He kept up the imperial dignity of his person to the height, and yet reigned in the hearts of his people, and swayed the world by their love to him, so that no Prince could be farther from deserving the name of a persecutor. Ammianus indeed objects that he took off his uncles, and prosecuted his victory over Magnentius too far ; but he did the first because they poisoned his father and the last, to secure not himself but Christianity from the attempts of the heathens. And these objections being removed, the character which Ammianus gives of him is great, and agrees with that of Hilary, Libanius and Gregory Nazianzen. And if these four witnesses suffice not, let me add a fifth. For Epiphanius (Haeres. 69, sect. 12) saith that he was merciful and good and pious in all respects as the son of the great and perfect and pious Constantine, this one thing excepted, that by the influence of his bishops he erred in the faith.

All these witnesses lived in the reign of this Emperor, and therefore knew what they wrote, and being his enemies would not favour him ; for they wrote after his death, and so were at liberty to speak their minds.[1]

---

[1] Another sentence is added in pencil (? by Conduitt) " and therefore if any later author affirms the contrary he ought to be corrected."

THE LANGUAGE OF THE PROPHETS

PREFACE

"The First Book Concerning the Language of the Prophets" contains about 50,000 words on 152 pp., and, though complete in itself, is apparently only the first part of a larger project.

Here is given the first Chapter and the headings of the remaining eight chapters. Chapter Five is divided into five sections, of which the sub-titles of sections III and IV are significant—" Of the Division of Empire and Church into Two Empires and Two Churches " and " A Further Account of the Division of the Roman Empire."

The first Chapter indicates the author's general view of prophetic interpretation and the titles of the following chapters give the subjects upon which he exercised his art.

[THE LANGUAGE OF THE PROPHETS]

1. *A Synopsis of the Prophetic Figures*

HE that would understand a book written in a strange language must first learn the language, and if he would understand it well must learn the language perfectly. Such a language was that wherein the Prophets wrote, and the want of sufficient skill in that language is the main reason why they are so little understood. John did not write in one language, Daniel in another, Isaiah in a third and the rest in others peculiar to themselves, but they all write in one and the same mystical language, as well known without doubt to the sons of the Prophets as the Hieroglyphic language of the Egyptians to their priests. And this language, so far as I can find, was as certain and definite in its signification as is the vulgar language of any nation whatsoever, so that it is only through want of skill therein that Interpreters so frequently turn the Prophetic types and phrases to signify whatever their fancies and hypotheses lead them to. He therefore that would understand the old

Prophets (as all Divines ought to do) must fix the signification
of their types and phrases in the beginning of his studies. Something in the kind has been done by former writers ; and as
I have endeavoured in the following discourse to carry on
the design further, so I hope others will bring it to more
perfection. The Rule I have followed has been to compare
the several mystical places of scripture where the same prophetic
phrase or type is used, and to fix such a signification to that
phrase as agrees best with all the places : and, if more significations than one be necessary, to note the circumstances by which
it may be known in what signification the phrase is taken in any
place : and, when I had found the necessary, significations, to
reject all others as the offspring of luxuriant fancy, for no more
significations are to be admitted for true ones than can be
proved. And as Critics for understanding the Hebrew consult
also other oriental languages of the same root ; so I have not
feared sometimes to call in to my assistance the Eastern
expositors of their mystical writers (I mean the Chaldee
Paraphrast and the Interpreters of dreams) following herein
the example of Mr. Mede and other late writers. For the
language of the Prophets, being Hieroglyphical, had affinity
with that of the Egyptian priests and Eastern wise men, and
therefore was anciently much better understood in the East
than it is now in the West. I received also much light in this
search by the analogy between the world natural and the world
politic. For the mystical language was founded in this analogy,
and will be best understood by considering its original. That
you may therefore see more clearly how this analogy stands I
shall here give you a short draught of it as follows before I proceed to the proof of the particulars.

1. The whole world natural consisting of heaven and earth
signifies the whole world politic consisting of thrones and people,
or so much of it as is considered in the prophecy ; and the
things in that world signify the analogous things in this. For
the Heavens with the things therein signify thrones and dignities
and those that enjoy them, and the earth with all the things

therein the inferior people, and the lowest parts of the earth, called Hades or Hell, the lowest and most miserable part of the people. Whence, ascending towards heaven and descending to the earth is put for rising and falling in honour and power. Rising out of the earth or waters, or falling into them, for the rising to any dominion or dignity out of the inferior state of people, or falling from the same into that inferior state. Descending into the lower parts of the Earth called Hades or Hell, for descending to a very low and unhappy state. Speaking with a faint voice out of the dust for being in a weak and low condition. Moving from one place to another for translation from one office, dignity or dominion to another. Great earthquakes and the shaking of heaven and earth for the shaking of kingdoms so as to overthrow them. The creating a heaven and earth and their passing away, or, which is all one, the beginning and end of the world—for the rise and ruin of the body politic signified thereby.

2. Now in heaven the Sun and Moon are by Interpreters of dreams put for the persons of Kings and Queens, but in sacred Prophecy, which regards not single persons, the Sun is put for the whole species and race of Kings in the Kingdom or Kingdoms of the world politic shining with regal power and glory : the Moon for the body of the common people considered as the King's wife : the stars for subordinate Kings, Princes and great men, or for Bishops and Rulers of the people of God when the Sun is Christ : Light—for the glory, truth and knowledge wherewith great and good men shine and illuminate others : Darkness—for obscurity of conditions and for error and ignorance : darkening, smiting or setting of the Sun, Moon and stars—for the ceasing of a kingdom or for the desolation thereof proportional to the darkness : darkening the Sun, turning the Moon into blood and falling of stars—for the same. New Moons—for the return of a dispersed people into a body politic or ecclesiastic.

3. Fire and Meteors refer to both heaven and earth and signify as follows. Burning anything by fire is put for the

i

consumption thereof by war : a conflagration of the earth or
turning a country into a lake of fire—for the consumption of a
kingdom by war : the being in a furnace—for the being in
slavery under another nation : the ascending up of the smoke
of any burning thing for ever and ever—for the continuation of
a conquered people under the misery of perpetual subjection
and slavery : the scorching heat of the Sun—for vexatious war,
persecutions and troubles inflicted by the king. Clouds,
whether in heaven or on earth—for multitudes of men : Riding
on the clouds—for reigning over much people : Covering the
Sun with a cloud or with smoke—for oppression of the king by
the armies of an enemy : Tempestuous winds (that is, the
motion of clouds)—for wars : Thunder (that is, the voice of a
cloud)—for the voice of a multitude : A storm of thunder,
lightning, hail and overflowing rain—for a tempest of war
descending from the heavens and clouds politic on the heads of
their enemies. Rain, if not immoderate, and dew, and living
water—for the graces and doctrine of the spirit, and the defeat
of rain—for spiritual barrenness.

4. In earth the dry land and congregated waters (as a Sea,
a River, a Flood) are put for the peoples of several regions,
nations, and dominions : embittering of waters—for great
afflictions of the people by war and persecution : turning them
into blood—for the mystical death of bodies politic, that is, for
their dissolution. The overflowing of a Sea or River—for
the invasion of the earth politic by the people of the waters.
Drying up of waters—for the conquest of their regions by the
earth : fountains of water—for cities the permanent heads of
rivers politic. Mountains and Islands—for the cities of the earth
and sea politics with their territories and dominions. Dens
and Rocks of mountains—for the Temples of Cities ; and the
hiding of men in those Dens and Rocks—for the shutting up of
Idols in their temples. Houses and ships—for family assemblies
and towns in the earth and sea politic ; and a navy of warships—
for an army of the kingdom signified by the sea.

5. Also Animals, Vegetables, and Minerals are put for people of several regions and conditions ; and particularly trees, herbs, and land animals—for the peoples of the earth politic, flags, reeds and fishes for those of the waters politic, and birds and insects for those of the politics, heaven and earth ; a forest for a Kingdom, Paradise for a very flourishing and peaceable kingdom, and a Wilderness for a desolate and their people.

6. If the world politic considered in Prophecy consists of many kingdoms, they are represented by as many parts of the world natural : as the noblest by the celestial frame, and then the Moon and clouds are put for the common people ; the less noble by the earth, sea, and rivers and by the animals or vegetables or buildings therein, and then the greater and more powerful animals and taller trees are put for Kings and Princes. And because the whole kingdom is the body politic of the King, therefore the Sun or a Tree or a Beast or Bird or Man, whereby the king is represented, is put in a large signification for the whole kingdom, and several animals as a Lion, a Goat, a Dragon, a Whore, a Prophet, a Frog, a Cherubim, according to their qualities, are put for several kingdoms and bodies politic, and sacrificing of Beasts for slaughtering and conquering of Kingdoms, and friendships between Beasts for peace between Kingdoms. Yet sometimes Vegetables and Animals are by certain epithets or circumstances extended to other significations, as a Tree, when called the tree of life or of knowledge, and a Beast when called the old Serpent, or worshipped.

7. When a Beast or Man is put for a kingdom, his parts and qualities are put for the analogous parts and qualities of the Kingdom as the head of a Beast for the great men who precede and govern ; the tail for the inferior people who follow and are governed, the heads, if more than one, for the number of capital parts, dynasties or dominions in the kingdom, whether collateral or successive with respect to the civil government : the horns on any head for the number of kingdoms in that head with

respect to military power : seeing—for understanding, and the eyes—for men of understanding and policy ; and, in matters of religion—for Bishops : Speaking—for making laws, and the mouth—for a lawgiver, whether civil or sacred : the loudness of the voice—for might and power ; the faintness thereof—for weakness ; eating and drinking—for acquiring what is signified by the things eaten and drunken : the hairs of a Beast as Man and the feathers of a Bird—for people : the wings—for the branches of a people spread abroad by conquest over other nations : the arm of a man—for his power or for any people wherein his strength and power consists : his feet— for the lowest of the people or for the latter end of the kingdom : the feet, nails and teeth of a Beast of prey—for armies and squadrons of armies : the bones—for strength and fortified places : the flesh—for riches and possessions, and the days of their continuing or acting—for years. And when a Tree is put for a kingdom its branches, leaves and fruit signify as to the wings, feathers and food of a Bird.

8. When a man is taken in a mystical sense, his qualities are often signified by his actions and by the circumstances of things about him. So a Ruler is signified by his riding on a Beast : a Warrior and Conqueror by his having a sword and bow, a potent man by his gigantic stature ; a Judge by weights and measures, a sentence of absolution or condemnation by a white or black stone ; a new dignity by a new name ; moral and civil qualifications by garments ; honour and glory by splendid apparel ; royal dignity by purple or scarlet, or by a crown ; righteousness by white and clean robes ; wickedness by spotted and filthy garments ; affliction, mourning, and humiliation by clothing in sackcloth ; dishonour, shame, and want of good works by nakedness ; error and misery by drinking a cup of his or her wine who causes it ; propagating any religion—for gain by exercising traffic and merchandise with that people whose religion it is ; worshipping or serving the false gods of any nation by committing adultery with their

Princes or by worshipping them and their image and blaspheming God, or by receiving their mark or name or the number thereof in the hand or forehead in token of servitude ; overthrow in war by a wound of Man or Beast ; a durable plague of war by a sore and pain ; the affliction or persecution which a people suffer in labouring to bring forth a new Kingdom— by pain in travail of a man-child ; the birth of a new Kingdom by the birth of a man-child ; the dissolution of a body politic or ecclesiastic by the death of Man or Beast ; and the revival of a dissolved dominion by the resurrection of the dead.

9. Sometimes a body politic is represented by the building of a City or Temple, and then the stones of the building are put for the people of the Kingdom, and if the building be a City the walls, gates, windows and streets thereof have the same signification with the bones, heads, eyes, and body of the Beast ; and the regular and accurate structure of the city and its height and ornaments of gold, pearls, precious stones and other things of value denote the justice, height and glory of its dominion, but if it be a Temple the parts thereof have the same signification with the analogous parts of the world. For Temples were anciently contrived to represent the frame of the Universe as the true Temple of the great God. Heaven is represented by the Holy Place, or main body of the edifice, the highest heaven by the most Holy, or Adytum ; the throne of God by the Ark, the Sun by the bright flame of the fire of the Altar, or by the face of the Son of Man shining through this flame like the Sun in his strength ; the moon by the burning coals upon the Altar, convex above and flat below, like an half moon, the stars by the lamps, thunder by the song of the Temple, lightning by the flashing of the fire of the Altar, the Angels or inhabitants of heaven by Cherubims carved round the Temple, the Sea by the great brazen laver, the earth by the area of the Courts, and the bottomless pit, or lower parts of the earth called Hades and Hell, by the sink which ran down into the earth from the great Altar, and was crowned

with a stone to open and shut. And all these parts of the Temple have the same signification with the parts of the world which they represent. And, in allusion to the River Siloam which ran by the Temple of Jerusalem and flowed thence eastward, and was by the Jewish Doctors accounted a type of the Spirit ; a River of life flowing eastward from the throne of God with trees of life growing on the banks thereof is put for the Law of God going out from the Throne of the Kingdom to the Nations, the fruit of the trees and the waters of the River being that spiritual meat and drink which Christ has represented by his body and blood, and by the bread and wine in the Eucharist ; which were also prefigured by the Manna and rock of water in the wilderness.

Chapter 2. The Daily Worship described.

Chapter 3. The Prophecy of opening the sealed Book and of sounding the Trumpets described.

Chapter 4. The prophecy of the eaten Book described.

Chapter 5. Of the Kingdoms and Churches which are the subject of sacred Prophecy.

Chapter 6. The Prophecy of the Epistles to the seven Churches described.

Chapter 7. The Prophecy of opening the first six Seals explained.

Chapter 8. The Prophecy of opening the seventh Seal explained.

Chapter 9. The Prophecy of the three Woes at the voices of the three last Trumpets explained.

COMMON PLACE BOOK

PREFACE

The Common Place Book is a folio volume bound in limp vellum, with entries in English and Latin on 104 pages ; the rest, 220 pp., are blank, save for occasional subject headings. No entry is dated, but differences of ink and script indicate that the Book was used over a considerable period. The edges of some pages are rotted and a number of passages are illegible.

Page 1 has a single note at the top under the heading " Sentences." " A man may imagine things that are false, but he can only understand things that are true, for if the things be false, the apprehension of them is not understanding."

The next page contains index of Contents, a list of Historical writers, 73 in number, and against some of the names is the note " Trin. Coll.", followed by a shelf-mark.

There follows a list of " Authores Notandi " which include Lightfoot's *Horae Hebraicae et Talmudicae in universum Novum Testamentum*, and works on the " Kabbala," " Sohar," and rabbinical commentaries.

Other entries are under the following headings :—

1. " *Out of* Lord Falkland's *Discourse of Infallibility* " [1651].
   " Out of the Jesuit's Answer."
   " The Lord Falkland's Reply."
   " Out of Lord Falkland's Reply."

2. " Out of Lord George Digby's Letter to Sir Kenelm Digby."
   " Out of Sir Kenelm's Reply."
   " Out of Lord Digby's Answer."
   [From *Letters between the Lord George Digby and Sir Kenelm Digby Knt. concerning Religion* (1651) in which Lord George attacks the Roman church and his kinsman defends it.]

3. Observations upon Athanasius's Works.

4. De Antechristo.

5. On I John v, 7, 8.

6. De Millennio ac die Judiciis.

7. Of Innovations and the authors thereof.

8. Miscellanies [mainly extracts from early Christian writers].

9. De Trinitate [also on a later page].

10. De Monachis.

11. Interpretationes sacrarum literarum.   [Continued on a later
page].

12. De Bestia Bicorni.   [Also on a later page].

13. De Politia Ecclesiastica.

14. De Athanasio et Antonio.

15. Ad historiam Ecclesiasticam sub Constantino et Constantio.
spectantia.
Ad Historiam Ecclesiasticam sub Valente et Theolosio
spectantia.
Historia Ecclesiastica post tempora Theodosii.

16. De Arrianis et Eunomiansis et Macedoniansis.

17. De Patribus scriptoribus, Conciliis et Authoritate.

18. De Heresibus et Hereticis.

19. Ex Petavii Dogmatis Theologicis.   Tract I.

20. De Synodi Sardicensi et Ariminansi.

21. De nominibus Dei.

22. De Deo Uno.

23. Variantes Lectiones sacrarum literarum notandae.   Rom. VII.
25 ; I John iii, 16 ; I John v, 6 ; I John v, 7, 8 ; I Tim. iii.

24. Ex historia Ingulphi., edit. Oxoniis, 1684.

25. De Homousio, Hypostasi, substantia et personis.

Beginning at the other end of the Book are passages from the Bible,
with occasional comments thereon, under various headings :—

Mores Gentium ; Religio Ethica ; Idolatria ; Deus Pater ; Deus
Filius ; Christ's Incarnatio, Passio, Satisfactio, et Redemptio ;
Spiritus Sanctus Deus ; Angeli boni et mali ; Predestinatio. Many
items throughout the Book are brief notes on subjects discussed
elsewhere. Here a selection only is given.

Observations upon Athanasius' Works

[Part of this article is so faded as to be indecipherable.]

In all Athanasius' writings which he wrote before the reign of Julius the Apostate there is not the least mention of a human soul in Christ distinct from the Logos. And in divers of these works he insists much upon the incarnation [citations follow]. [Continuing in Latin, he says] I marvel that before Julian's time he wrote nothing of the soul [anima] of Christ, for Arius and his party always denied it, asserting that the Logos was capable of suffering. Nay all the world was of this opinion, for the Apollinarians were openly teaching it and also the Macedonians. Even Athanasius himself up to the time of Julian seems to have been of this mind, for in many places where the subject seemed to require that he should name the soul he speaks only of the body. For when the Arians raised this objection " If the Son is equal to the Father, how can he become man?" Athanasius did not reply "It was effected by the incarnation of a mediating human soul, but finds an answer without mention of a soul;" he proceeds indeed as though wishing to exclude the soul :—" The Word was made flesh and dwelt among us. He was made man and did not come into man." He adds a reason :—" Certain it is that if we say he came into man, we fall into the heresy of those who say " The Word descended into the son of Mary.' " Then, by way of explaining the true incarnation, he continues :—" The Word, when flesh was assumed, was made man for us, as Peter testifies, ' Christ having suffered in the flesh for us.' " Moreover it should be noticed that Athanasius employed expressions that excluded a human son, i.e. " body of a man " " human body " etc. Finally, Arians and all the world (Eusebians, Eunomians, Macedonians, and Apollinarians) are of this opinion, but yet it is not in dispute before the time of Julian. Clearly, Athanasius was held in restraint by this argument : " If the Word is equal to the Father, how was he made capable of suffering?" When the answer was given "By reason of the body," this could hardly be aptly defended, since the body is not the principle (principium) of feeling but an organ of sensations, so at length he found himself compelled to introduce a human soul to which sensations could be referred .... Observe that the distinction between " ousia " and " hypostasis " did not begin to be acquired before the time of Julian (Orat. conti. Arianos. Tom. i p. 519 C.D., 520 A.B.)

[Citations are given from Athanasius. On the Holy Trinity Dial. i ; Dionysius of Alexandria. Letter against Paul of Samosata, Reply to Question 7 ; Theophylact. Commentary on Philipp. ii, 6 ; also Oecumenius on same passage. Theodoret, Cyril of Alexandria, and Chrysostom]

[Appended is a discussion of Philippians ii, 6 : " Who being in the form of God thought it not robbery to be equal with God", which Mrs. Conduitt included amongst the MSS. to be published.]

[The crucial words ἴσα θεῷ are discussed in some detail.] In Job x, c =like " instar Deo " or " tamquam Deus " or " quasi Deus " " as a God."

Rapine must here be applied to something which is capable of rapine, that is, not to the substance or essence of a raptor or non-raptor, but to something that is acquirable by him. For the substance, essence or internal nature of a man is without the limits of what he may commit rapine in. As it is improper to call anything blind which is incapable of seeing, so it is improper to say anything is not acquired by rapine which is not acquirable by rapine. And therefore τὸ εἶναι ἴσα θεῷ [AV. to be equal with God] is to be understood not of the congenit or natural Divinity of the Saviour, but his glory and exaltation which he acquired by his death—which Paul expresses in the next words : " God highly exalted him and gave him a name above every name." He was a son before his incarnation, but he was made heir. The sense of the place is therefore " Let this mind be in you which was in Christ, who being now in form or state as or God, did not acquire by rapine or violence this being as a God, but by humbling himself and taking upon him the form or state of a man, suffering on the Cross that at his name every knee should bow . . . and that every tongue should confess that Jesus Christ is Lord to the glory of God the Father." Deity and worship are relative terms ; ἴσα θεῷ I understand not of what our Saviour has not, but of what he has, because it transcends not what he has. I understand it not of his congenit divinity, but of that exaltation to honour and dominion after his death which St. Paul describes in the following words. And for these two reasons, first, because the rapine must here be meant of something to which 'tis not incongruous yet to something which is some way or other acquirable. The substance or essence of a thing is not of those things acquirable by it, but of the very thing itself, and it would be improper to speak of rapine about things where rapine cannot, without an extravagant thought, come into consideration. This would be as improper as to call anything blind which is not capable of seeing. Secondly, οὐκ ἁρπαγμὸν ἡγήσατο τὸ εἶναι ἴσα θεῷ is as much as to say ἡγήσατο τὸ εἶναι ἴσα θεῷ οὐκ ἁρπαγμόν for τὸ εἶναι ἴσα θεῷ and οὐκ ἁρπαγμόν are two substantives in analogy with one another and both alike referred to ἡγήσατο.

[Following a discussion of " Antichrist " are two notes in different ink and slightly larger script]

" In Queen Mary's reign, in a little above 5 years time there were according to the truest account, no fewer than 284 Protestants burnt at stake for professing the Gospel, besides those that died in prison or were exiled. Nay, the author of the preface to Bishop Ridley's book " De coena Domini," who is commonly supposed to have been Grindal, that was afterwards Archbishop of Canterbury—a person who by his circumstances and troubles in the time of that bloody reign, and by his station and quality under Queen Elizabeth, had as fair advantage as any of being informed concerning the number of those that suffered—tells us there were above eight hundred put to most cruel kinds of death for religion in the two first years of Queen Mary's persecution." " *No Protestant Plot*, Part 3ᵈ, page 3."

" Aeneas Sylvius, who afterwards was Pius ii, gave this

character to the Popedom, that there was never any great slaughter in Christendom, nor any great calamity happened either of Church or State, whereof the Bishops of Rome were not the Authors. *Hist. Austria.* And as much is said by Machiavelli in his *History of Florence*, Reflections on the Roman Clergy, at the end of the Politics of France.' "

On I John V, 7, 8.

" There are three that bear record in heaven, the Father, the word and the holy spirit, and these three are one.[1] Those of greater note, learning and caution, as Grotius, Erasmus, and Luther (in his edition of the New Testament) read this place thus : " There are three that bear record, the spirit, the water and the blood, and these three are one " (or into one thing), only Grotius leaves out " these three are one."[2] And justly do they ; for first a great part, if not the greater part of the Greek manuscripts read it thus, and especially the ancienter, as the Alexandrine sent to King Charles 1st by the patriarch of Constantinople, and supposed to be written by Thecla, of whom Eusebius writes (Lib. 8, Hist.) as being martyred before the Council of Nice ; the capital letters 'tis wrote in and other signs arguing its great antiquity. Secondly, it was not in the copies in use in the Church in the time of Constantine the Great and his sons. . . . That which Gregory Nazianzen used, for when his adversaries pleaded that the father and son were not two Gods, because things of a different essence are not connumerated, Nazianzen answers that St. John (I John, 5) connumerates things which are not co-essential, saying : " There are three that bear record, the spirit, the water and the blood " (Oratio 37 " De Spiritu Sancto "). Since he quotes this only and not the other part—" There are three which bear record in heaven, the Father, the word, and the Spirit—

[1] Cp. 1 John v, 7. " For there are three that bear record in heaven, the Father, the Word, and the Holy Ghost, and these three are one."

[2] Cp. 1 John v, 8 (A.V.). " And there are three that bear witness in earth, the spirit, and the water, and the blood : and these three agree in one."

which would have been much more to his purpose, as being an instance of connumeration of the very things in dispute. And besides he leaves out the words ' on earth,' which used not to be left out where the three in heaven are put. It is plain this other part was not in the copy he used. Further, that ancient MS. of Lincoln College in Oxford and those of Magdalen and New College have it not—nor the MS. of Grotius supposed by him to be of a 1,000 years antiquity. The Syriac, Arabic and Ethiopic versions, which are very ancient, want it, and so did all the Latin versions in Jerome's time, as Jerome himself mentions. Cyril of Alexandria also (Thesaurus, Assert. 34 sub finem) cites the place at large without it. Oecumenius, in his comment on the place, has it not. The copies of the Eunomians had it not, for they objected that the spirit was nowhere joined with the father and son but in baptism. (See Basil contr. Eunom. lib. c.). The copy of Basil had it not, for though he disputes largely for the trinity and the divinity of the holy ghost both in his book ' Contr. Eunom.' and in ' Ad Amphilochium,' and brings all the arguments he could rap [?wrap], and read together, yet he mentions not this place ; no, not in that chapter where he answers the Eunomians' aforesaid objections. And for the same reason the copy of Athanasius and Gregory Nazianzen had it not : nor that of Didymus Alexandrinus, who wrote a particular tract about the Holy Ghost to prove out of Scripture his divinity and union with the Father and Son, and also wrote a commentary on St. John's Epistles, and yet has not this place. Epiphanius also wrote professedly to prove the Trinity, and yet has not this place, nor Chrysostom, Theodoret, Damascene, or any other ancient Greek writer. Oecumenius in his comment on this place has it not . . . "

[In what follows there is little not given more fully in the first part of *An Historical Account of Two Notable Corruptions of Scripture*, of which this is an early rough draft. That Treatise, however, does not mention Christopher Sand's *Interpretationes Paradoxae Quatuor Evangeliorum*, 1669, here cited for its evidence of the reading in an Armenian MS. found by Sand at Amsterdam. Probably the omission was due to Sand's well-known heretical opinions. The Treatise, too, omits reference to the Sermon by Thomas Smith, Fellow of Magdalen College, Oxford, on *The Credibility of the Mysteries of the Christian Religion*, 1675, which, named towards the end of this MS., may provide a clue to the approximate date of Newton's composition of this draft of the discussion of the first text, I John v, 7, 8.

Here it is proper to consider " Deus Filius," a MS. note of some five pages, consisting of pertinent New Testament texts with marginal readings from other sources e.g. Aquila on Psalm vii. In the margin opposite I Tim. iii, 16 (" God was manifest in the flesh " A.V.) evidence is given for the reading " he who " instead of " God " and also the readings in Erasmus, Grotius, the Polyglot etc. It forms, indeed, a brief, rough draft of Newton's later composition—the discussion of the second of the texts in the Treatise published anonymously in 1754 and by Bishop Horsley in his edition of Newton's *Works*, vol. v, 1785. In the later edition Newton frequently admits that the reading of the masculine relative, and not only the neuter, as in the earlier edition, may have been in the Greek text of Latin authors cited.

It is an evidence (one of many) that he continued to work on the Treatise after he sent a copy to Locke, and of his single-minded desire to seek the truth. The masculine is adopted by most modern editions and translators, including the Revised Versions (English and American). The difference between the three readings in dispute, " Which," " Who," and " God " is in the original that between O, OC, and ΘC. The change of the second to the third form is the easiest of any possible mutation of letters].

DE MILLENNIO AC DIE JUDICE

[The traditional chronology, based on Scripture, which makes one day equal to a thousand years, provides the foundation on which the Millennium and the Day of Judgment are discussed. Hence, " the creation," we learn, " occupied a period of 6,000 years."

[Quotations from the Vulgate and Septuagint are numerous. The Epistle of Barnabas is cited as the work of a companion of St. Paul.]

" Let no man judge you in meat or in drink or in respect of an holy day or of the new Moon, or of the Sabbath days ; which are a shadow of things to come." Coloss. ii, 16, viz. A holy day of the great and final holy day, the new Moon of the renovation or refreshment or new creation of all things, and the Sabbath of the seventh thousand year, the great day of rest. [Hebrews iv, 1-4, is then cited.]   Of all the heathens Lactantius is witness that the most ancient and famous writers—Hydaspis, King of the Medes, Mercurius Trismegistus and the Sybils—determined and confirmed this duration of the world. [Hilary, Jerome, Augustine, Irenaeus, Papias, Tertullian and Justus Martyr are cited, and stress laid upon Daniel vii, 25 and viii, 14 and passages in Isaiah. For the conflict of Gog and Magog, reference is made to Targum Megilla ii, 12, Abenezra and Saadia ; and finally Grotius on the Apocalypse showing that their interpretation of the two resurrections and the millennium and New Jerusalem are incorrect] which " gave occasion to many for the rejection of the Apocalypse as the work of Corinthus or another Judaizer."

Of Innovators and the Authors thereof

The superstitions of the Cross and Chrism were in use in the second century. The Millennary error got footing about that time ; the necessity of Infants receiving the blessed sacrament of the Lord's Supper came in soon after. About the 4th century these were some touches in oratory sermons by way of Rhetoric, ejaculations like praying to the saints, but long after came to be formally used as now in churches. . . .

Those foreheads which the sign of God had purified (viz. in baptismal ablutions and confirmation) abhorred the garlands of Satan, and reserved themselves to be crowned by God (Cyprian, De Laps. in principia).

Damasus [Pope 366-384], in order that the Psalms might be sung in turn in Church, placed at the end of each, " Glory to the Father, and to the Son, and to the Holy Ghost." He first gave authority to the writings of Jerome. The singing of Psalms day and night was instituted by Damasus, says Anastasius in his life—I suppose alternately by turn and in all public assemblies, for privately, at least, if not in some churches, they were sometimes sung earlier, though possibly not in this manner. Besides it is certain that in the time of Cassianus (i.e. 50 years after Damasus) Gloria Patri etc. was not sung at the end of Psalms in Eastern churches (see Cassian, Lib. ii De nocturn. Orat. mod. c.B) . . . Silvester, in whose time the Synod of Nicea met, instituted the consecration of Chrism by the Bishop, the signing of baptized with the sign of a cross, and anointing him with chrism, the wearing of the surplice by deacons in the church, of a linsey-wolsey cloak or hood upon their left shoulder, and the exemption of the clergy from lay accusations or judicature, and the celebration of the mass in a linen surplice . . .

Felix, who began in 272, appointed that masses should be celebrated over the sepulchres of martyrs . . . Alexander, who began 121, appointed the sprinkling of water with salt in the homes of the people (Anastas Quaes). . . .

Innocent, who began in 402, decreed that a fast should be observed on the Sabbath because on the Sabbath our Lord was placed in the Sepulchre, and his disciples fasted. [A long discussion follows on the vexed question in East and West of the re-baptism of heretics.]

Miscellanea

According to ancient tradition baptism was in the name of Christ. About baptizing, Tertullian, who knew well the custom of the ancient Church, teaches that in case of necessity, " Quilibet Laicus tingit." For the surplice the testimonies of Chrysostom and Jerome that the priests in the ancient Church officiated in white vestments are well enough known.

In the Council of Nice when it was debated whether married Priests should be separated from their wives and the major part were inclined to the wrong side, Paphnutius stood up and set them right, proving the ancient traditions or customs of the Church to the contrary.

The Nicene Fathers decreed that no bishop should have a wife. For from the time of the Apostles to the Council of Nice they had wives, Patriarchs excepted, and a married person [as such] was not denied the office. Eutych. Annal. p. 450, 451.

In the Chron. Alexr., after the Council of Nice, and some other things done in July and October in the 20th of Constantine, it is added towards the end of the year : Constantine slew Crispus Caesar, his son by Fausta, who was overcome by envy. (See Gothofred, " Comments in Cod. Third.")

Very many Christians under the Diocletian persecutions [begun 250 A.D.] fled to the Barbarians and were courteously received. (Eusebius in Vita Constaninus, Lib. III, c. 51, 52.)

There were prayers for the dead in Chrysostom's time. He was a believer in transubstantiation. (Chrysost. Hom. 32, 51) [John Chrystom ?347-407 A.D.]

De Politica Ecclesiastica
[An outline is given of the history of the Church in Alexandria from the ninth year of Claudius Ceasar, when Mark the evangelist invited men to put their faith in Christ our Lord . . . After a note stating that " Basil, Bishop of Caesarea had fifty bishops under him," it is added in English, " Thou shalt not follow a multitude to do evil." Exod. xxiii, 2.

[Two citations from Jerome are given on the equality of bishops and presbyters (dignity apart) and of the interchange of the terms in the Apostolic period.]

De Homousio, Ousia, Hypostasi Substantia et Personis
Jerome in his Epistle to Damaris (Epist. 57), scrupling at the use of three Hypostases, does notwithstanding expound sub-

K

stance of the genus and makes three hypostases to signify three
kinds of substances or ousias. Epiphanius (Haer., 69, 70),
making but one hypostasis in the Deity, at the same time
expounds it of the generical unity. So Athanasius with two
Councils of Alexandria, allowing the language of one hypostasis,
makes a general union and similitude of substance, as you may
see in the Epistle to the Antiocheans, p. 577, and that to the
Africans, p. 938 B.

That the churches in the times next after Constantius were
so far from making one singular substance that they decried it
for heresy and Sabellianism, notwithstanding any distinction of
persons whatever. See the Creed of Liberius sent to
Athanasius, and the Council of Alexandria's Epistle to the
Antiocheans in Athanasius, Tom. i, p 533 ; St. Basil Epistle 64,
p. 847, 848, 850, Epistle 78, p. 889 D, 890 A., Epistle 349,
p. 1129 D, 1130 A, Epistle 345, p. 1122 C., Epistle 391, p. 1172 ;
B. Hosius, Contr. Sabel. p. 601 ; Greg. Nazianz. Orat. 21, also
Epistle Concilii in civitate Francia ac Parisiis ; in Hilary
" Fragments " and Tom. i, Concil. Gallie. p. 16.

" The Homousios was condemned by the Council of Antioch
against Paul of Samosata." Basil. Epist. 300, p. 1069 B.

" Disputations about the Holy Ghost not moved till Basil's
time or a very little before Basil." Epistle 388, p. 1162 A.B.

De Synodo Sardicensi ac Ariminansi

That the Council of Sardica did write concerning the faith,
as 'tis recorded by Theodoret, contrary to Athanasius, appears
by the testimony of Sacbadius in Jerome, " De Script.
Ecclesiasticis in Sacbadio," and " apud Baronius, an. 357,
16," and perhaps by the testimony of Hilary, " contra Constantium p. 333 B."—" his verbis. Damnas quoque Substantiae
nomen quo et Sardicensi Synodo et Sermicensi piam esse
mentiebaris."

Christi Incarnatio

[After a cento of texts from both Testaments a note is added.]
" The Jews did not expect their Messiah to be more than a

man, yet freely called him the Son of God. Christ did not magnify his divinity before his passion, yet freely called himself the Son of God. See Matt. xxiv, 23, xxvii, 63, xxvii, 54.

[Scattered throughout the Book are isolated notes in Latin and English, often referring to books. Here are two, one in each tongue.]

" Liber diurnus Romanorum Pontificum." " From an ancient Codex MS., a work brought to light by the zeal of John Garner, priest, of the Society of Jesus, who added notes and dissertations in the year 1679. Paris. But on the title-page the year is given as 1680."

[The Common Place Book, pp. 111 f., has at the head of each page letters of the alphabet, A-Z., most of the pages contain no entry : L. and M. are here given.]

" Legends *vide* $\begin{matrix} \text{L.} \\ \text{M.} \end{matrix}$ Monks

" Monks. The legendary life of Hilary writ by Fortunatus in the beginning of his works."

[Fortunatus, Bishop of Poictiers (b. 530), was the author of eleven saints. Another Fortunatus (d. 569) is also credited with the first book of the life of Hilary and three other lives of saints.]

Idolatria

[Old Testaments passages are examined.] " Rachel and Laban were idolaters and yet worshipped the true God " ... " Idolatrous Egyptians and Israelites in Egypt acknowledged the true God." [One illustration is of interest for its application of reason and speculation in the attempt to elucidate the inspired text.]

" It is not probable that Solomon, to whom God appeared twice, I Kings ii, 9, and who was the wisest of men and understood the nature of all trees, fowls, creeping things and fishes, I Kings iv, 33, could be so little a Philosopher as to think that images made of gold, or wood, or stone were Deities. We may

K₁

rather suppose that he fell into idolatry through a persuasion that there was some reality in the supposed gods—Chemosh, Molech, Asteroth etc., to which the heathen idols were dedicated, and so worshipped these idols in respect to them. For if we consider that in the books of Moses and the Judges there is frequent mention of Angels employed on several occasions to execute the will of God in the government of the world, why might not his heathen wives and concubines, by telling him stories of the works and power of their gods, persuade him to think that the supreme God had committed the government of the world to Angels and such like intermediate beings, and that of this sort were the Heathen deities, and therefore might be worshipped as the superintendents of mankind ? And thus notwithstanding his wisdom, he might be persuaded to go a whoring after them, as he did. I Kings xi, 7, 3.

Interpretationes Sacrarum Literarum

" Of whom is Christ according to the flesh ὁ ὢν ἐπὶ πάντων θεὸς εὐλογητὸς εἰς τοὺς αἰῶνας, ἀμήν. He who is God over all be blessed for ever." Rom. ix, 5. So Erasmus ὁ is not a relative but the emphatic article referring to θεός. The objection is raised that the word ἔστι is wanting. But so also is it elsewhere in doxologies, e.g. 2 Macs. xv, 34; Gen. ix, 26, xxiv, 27; Exod. xviii, 10 ; Ruth iv, 14 ; I Kings i, 48, v, 7 ; viii, 15, 56 ; Ezra vii, 27 I Chrons. xvi, 36 ; Psal. xli, 13, lxxii, 18, 19, lxxxi, 52 and Ephes. i, 3 ; II Cor. i, 3 ; I Pet. i, 3.

The words therefore of Paul are a doxology of God according to the form current in the Jewish church from of old. That may be inferred also from the word "Amen," which is not placed at the end of a sentence except after a prayer. But Tertull. adv. Praxeas and Cyprian Lib. ii c. 6 have the reading of the common version. And it is said that κατὰ σάρκα and ὁ θεός are in opposition. But the sense after κατὰ σάρκα is complete, and opposition ought to be between " ex homine " and " ex Deo " as in Rom. i, 3-4, not between what is of man and the supreme God. Finally, when Paul introduced a malediction on his brethren and chose for himself to be accursed for his brethren's sake, he qualified his words with God's benediction. For men of piety are wont to bless when anything evil happens to themselves, but not to moderate their speech on matters evil like wicked men who, under punishment, bless the King. For Paul's practice, see in this same epistle i, 24, 25 and compare I Tim. i, 17.

Let it not seem difficult to begin a sentence with the article ὁ—nothing is more common,[1] and, when it relates to God, as in doxologies, the expression is emphatic. Cp Philip. iv, 19.

Ambrose gives evidence that some in his time referred the benediction here to God the Father. And it should be observed that Greeks distinguished periods in Paul's letters, according to the sense, in sections. This section they close with the words εὐλογητὸς εἰς τοὺς αἰῶνας, ἀμήν.

Certainly ὁ ὤν cannot refer to the preceding phrase except by apposition or as one substantive is wont to be opposed to another. If you want a relative it must be ὅς ἐστι or ὅς ὤν. not ὁ ὤν. Furthermore, as Paul concludes this section with this doxology, so he does other sections with other doxologies and prayers.[2]

---

[1] So Rom. ii, 21, 22, viii, 27 ; 1 Cor. vii, 22, 1 John ii, 4, 6, 9, 10, 11.

[2] At the end of Chap. xiv ancient MSS. rightly insert the three verses now read at the end of the Epistle.

GENERAL INDEX

SCRIPTURE INDEX

Date Due